DAVENPORT'S KANSAS WILLS AND ESTATE PLANNING LEGAL FORMS

written by attorneys
Alex Russell and Robert Maxwell

PUBLICATION DATA

(informal, library may use different data)

Names: Russell, Alex, 1972- author ; Maxwell, Robert, 1960- author

Title: Davenport's Kansas Wills And Estate Planning Legal Forms

Other Titles: Davenport's Wills

Description: Davenport Publishing 2023

Suggested Identifiers: 9798395858931, LCCN 2021909030, 9798748423373

Subjects: LCSH: Wills--United States;
                   Wills--United States--Forms;
                   Estate Planning--United States;
                   Legal Forms

Classification: LFF KF755 .C55 2022 (or as library chooses)
                   DDC 346.73 Rus--dc23 (or as library chooses)

9 8 7 6 5 4 3 2 1 0 0 0 0 0 2 3

BOOKS AND FORMS FOR OTHER STATES ARE AVAILABLE, SEE <u>WWW.DAVENPORTPUBLISHING.COM</u> FOR INFORMATION

CHAPTER	TABLE OF CONTENTS	PAGE NUMBER

WILL RELATED FORMS

HEALTH CARE FORMS

GIVING POWER FORMS

CHAPTER 1
BOOK BASICS AND LIST OF FORMS

ESTATE PLANNING CONTROLS THINGS IF LATER ABSENT, SICK, OR DEAD

From Davenport Publishing and written by attorneys this book is on "Estate Planning", about doing legal documents to control health care, property, money, children, funeral, and more if later absent, sick, or dead. People have a legal right to control their health care, property, money, and family issues, and so judges, doctors, and other people mostly just ask: "Based on what a person wrote what did they likely want done?"

ESTATE PLANNING MOSTLY IS DOING SIMPLE THINGS IN 3 AREAS

Estate Planning is mostly doing simple things in 3 areas: Will Related, Health Care, and Giving Power. There are 9 ready to use legal forms for Kansas in this book. Many people use just 1 to 3 legal forms.

WILL RELATED FORMS

Form 1. Will (Standard) – a Will (also called a "Last Will And Testament") lets a person control things after their death like who gets money and property, who is Executor, and if easier legal options can be used.

Form 2. Will (Guardian) – Will with part added to name someone to if needed be Guardian to care for a minor child under 18 (like if no parent is available) and be Conservator to manage their money and property.

Form 3. Self-Proving Affidavit – form sometimes done with Will to help prove it was properly signed.

Form 4. Tangible Personal Property List – lets person easily add to a Will more gifts to occur after death of tangible personal property like furniture, jewelry, vehicles, art, electronics, tools, and clothes.

HEALTH CARE FORMS

Form 5. Durable Power Of Attorney For Health Care Decisions – lets a person name someone to be Agent to control health care if the person is ever incapacitated and also give some health care instructions.

Form 6. Living Will Declaration – lets a person do serious act of saying stop most health care if later they are incapacitated and doctors think the health situation is very bad and more care likely won't help.

Form 7. Pre-hospital Do Not Resuscitate Request – does very serious act of saying immediately from now on don't try resuscitation including C.P.R. (cardio-pulmonary resuscitation) if heart or breathing stops.

GIVING POWER FORMS

Form 8. General Durable Power Of Attorney – lets power over money, property, and more be given to trusted person so they have power to do things, like use accounts, pay bills, get records, and sell property.

Form 9. Durable Power Of Attorney For Health Care And Education (About Children) – lets parent of a child under 18 share power with someone over the child's health care and school decisions.

KANSAS LAW ON ESTATE PLANNING COVERS MOST PEOPLE IN THE STATE

This book is for Kansas only since Estate Planning law and legal documents are different in each state. Whether local Estate Planning law applies is based on a person's primary residence (often called "domicile"). Many judges say residence occurs if a person lives in a place and for a moment has no clear plans to leave. Later plans to move don't matter till people actually move. People can stay under a state's Estate Planning laws even if they leave a state if living elsewhere is temporary and people always have firm plans to return. For example some people who leave for months or more for travel, for school, for special work projects, and the military may qualify to keep ties to their old state. Immigrants of any kind can do normal Estate Planning. For health care people often do legal documents to match the state a hospital or other health facility is in.

BOOK IS SHORT, HAS FORMS TO QUICKLY SEE, AND USES EMPHASIS

This book is short and may read rough but can be read fast. Long books often lead to misunderstanding of the basics and skimming. This book has legal forms people can quickly see. For emphasis paragraph titles, underlining, and boxes are used. This book capitalizes some legal words like Will, Testator, and Agent but this is optional. To save space some small words are skipped and end quote marks put before punctuation.

THIS BOOK COVERS MAJOR LEGAL IDEAS AND SHOULD SUIT MOST PEOPLE

This book covers the big U.S. legal ideas on Estate Planning and most ways Kansas state law is different. This book and its forms can't cover every issue that matters to everyone but it should suit people without any strange situations or wishes about Estate Planning, which is likely most adults (maybe well over 80%). Strange situations or wishes that may need more research or a lawyer include: a) unusual wishes for gifts, b) wealth over $5 million, c) big medical concerns including extreme age, d) property or money going to a person with disability or special needs, and e) wish to move or hide assets to qualify for government help.

LEGAL FORMS CAN HELP AND THIS BOOK PROVIDES "STANDARD FORMS"

Studies on Estate Planning show a surprising 60% of adults have not done anything, 19% used a lawyer for this, and 21% used legal forms. Legal forms are good at most things involved in Estate Planning and can make binding legal documents that judges, doctors, families, banks, and others legally must follow. Instead of legal forms a lawyer can be used for Estate Planning but they can be costly, take months of work, and make mistakes. In life people often weigh costs, benefits, and risks and often choose a cheaper option. Also, often a hospital, state agency, charity, or state legislature has made a form most people use and call the "standard form", and doctors, judges, and others may not like to follow anything else including even if a lawyer wrote it. This book does provide the standard form for Kansas in a subject area if it exists.

ESTATE PLANNING OFTEN IS NOT VITAL AND WORTH SPENDING MUCH ON

Despite what many people think Estate Planning often does not greatly change the costs, taxes, delays, and work involved in these areas, so it often is not vital and worth spending much money and energy on. Benefits also seem low for some groups since only about 4% of people die by age 50, and only about 0.13% of children under 18 had both parents die to need big legal help. See Social Security Tables: Felicitie Bell; Parent Mortality Census SIPP Paper #288. Instead of costly Estate Planning buying life insurance may be a better use of money, and many people pay yearly for about $100,000 term life insurance.

LEGAL DOCUMENTS MAY NEED TO BE "WITNESSED" OR "NOTARIZED"

Legal documents may need to be "witnessed", which is someone watching the person doing a form sign and then they sign too. Documents may need to be "notarized", which is a person who is a "notary" (also called a "notary public") see signing and use ink stamp and then they sign too. Notaries are at some banks, brokers, insurance agents, courts, law offices, libraries, mailing or copying centers, and government offices, but they can be busy or only help current customers. A phonebook can help people find a helpful notary. If a person signs a legal document in a language they don't understand it is still usually valid and binding.

A PERSON EXECUTES, SUBSCRIBES, OR ACKNOWLEDGES A DOCUMENT

In legal documents the words "subscribe" or "execute" means a person signed it, and "acknowledgment" means a person somehow showed a 2nd person like a notary or a witness they intended to do a document. In legal documents the word "seal" may appear for traditional reasons even if a signature is all that is needed.

ANYONE CAN FILL IN MOST OF FORM, AND LATER TRY TO KEEP ORIGINAL

When filling out a legal form except for signatures other parts can be filled in by someone not doing the form with good handwriting or typing. After a form is done usually people try to keep the original and hand out copies. Some people have everyone sign multiple copies to have multiple copies with ink signatures.

SOME LESS COMMON OR LESS USEFUL FORMS ARE NOT IN THIS BOOK

This book skips some less common or less useful documents.

- A "Codicil" can modify a Will but it is easier and legally safer to just re-do a Will.
- Some people do a "Pet Trust" to help a pet, but it's easier to just give money in Will to person given a pet.
- Though separate forms exist most people handle Organ Donation in drivers license or state ID forms.
- Some people do a "Revocable Living Trust" so a Trust entity with Trustee holds property or money during their life however long, usually done to after death avoid small delay, costs, or work (by "avoiding probate"). This is rare as it requires immediately moving most of a person's things into a Trust causing maybe years of hassles, mostly for small later benefits for people who are probably happy to do later work to get some things.
- "Childrens Trust" papers can be done (like in a Will) so a Trust at a death gets money or property for a minor child to manage until 18, but this is uncommon due to possible cost and hassles, since it rarely matters (as this book explains), and since most Wills already arrange other legal help for young children.

PROBABLY DO NEW FORMS IF DIVORCE, MARRY, HAVE CHILD, OR MOVE

Divorcing, marrying, having a new child, or moving to a new state can have big legal effects, and if any of these events occur it is recommended people do a new Will and other Estate Planning papers soon. To help most states say a Will from another state is still valid but this is not always certain.

NO FEDERAL OR KANSAS TAX IS USUALLY OWED DUE TO A DEATH

Usually no tax is owed as a result of a death, including no estate, inheritance, death, or similar taxes. This is because the Federal Estate And Gift Tax only starts when a tax credit is used up covering $13.99 million per person in 2025 and later. Kansas state no longer has an estate, inheritance, death, or similar tax. In rare cases a person or their estate here may owe a small amount for property in a different state.

CHAPTER 2
TERMS, PROPERTY LAW, AND HELPFUL INFORMATION FORM

THERE ARE BASIC TERMS AND IDEAS IN ESTATE PLANNING

Some legal terms and ideas are basic to Estate Planning.

■ "Estate Planning" is about people doing legal documents to control things if later absent, sick, or dead. After a document is done people are mostly free to sell or transfer property, instruct doctors, or change forms.

■ A "person doing a legal document" and "doing a form" means the form is for and affects that person.

■ A "Will" or "will" (this book uses upper case "W") is a legal document done to control issues after death. The phrase "Last Will And Testament" is used since a "Testament" long ago was a small document done along with a Will to do some things. If no Will is done a person is described as being "intestate".

■ A person who died is called the "decedent" or "deceased". A person getting a Will gift is called "recipient", "beneficiary", or "heir" if related (they "inherit"). "Survive" or "surviving" is to be alive after someone died.

■ A person named to handle and do things after someone's death is usually called an "Executor", but if a judge has to pick someone they are called an "Administrator". The term "Personal Representative" covers both these terms and is increasingly more often used in Kansas Wills and other papers.

■ A person doing a Will is called "Testator" or "Will maker". Before about 1990 a woman Testator was called a "Testatrix" and woman Executor called an "Executrix" but this is no longer often done.

■ "Probate" is a legal process to do things after someone's death like transfer property, handle creditors, and authorize a Guardian. Due to nice changes in law probate is now often informal, faster, and less costly.

■ "Property" is either: 1) "real property" which is land and buildings ("real estate"), 2) "personal property" which is things not real property, like cash, accounts, stocks, tools, clothes, cars, jewelry, and art, or 3) "fixtures" which are things tied to real property (like fences, posts, lighting, and wired-in appliances).

■ Legal documents to control health care things are often called "Advanced Directives".

■ In Kansas a person under 18 is usually called a "minor" and often a parent or guardian helps them. A minor or other person not reasonably able to make wise decisions lacks "capacity" and is "incapacitated".

■ Forms giving power to someone are often called "Power of Attorney" forms. The person giving power is called the "Principal" and person getting power is called the "Attorney-in-Fact" or "Agent".

■ State law is the "Kansas Statutes" which often are in books with notes called "annotations". A single law is called a "statute" or a "section" often shown by "§" or "s". Kansas law is divided in about 100 parts called "Chapters", for example Chapter 59 deals with Probate. A single Kansas law can be referred to in many different ways, like K.S. 59-606, K.S.A. 59-606, Kan. Stat. 59-606, or often Kansas Statutes 59-606. A legal form written in state law for people to find and use if wanted is usually called a "statutory form".

"ESTATE" MEANS PROPERTY OF DECEDENT OR ENTITY HOLDING ITEMS

The "Estate" or "probate estate" is all property and money of a dead person that at death or soon after did not somehow legally automatically transfer to other owners. "Estate" is also the word for the temporary entity run by an Executor to do things after a death (like a small corporation). A dead person's money and accounts might be renamed or moved to a bank under an Estate name, for example like "Estate of Ed Hud".

PERSON CAN ONLY GIFT IN WILL WHAT THEY OWN AT DEATH

A person can only gift by Will things they own at death <u>so people should research what they own</u>. Basically by law a person usually owns all they earn as wages and salary, owns their share of income and profit tied to property they own, and owns or partly owns any things their money buys or improves. And for property with "title" documents (real estate or vehicles) or where there is a "listed owner" (like accounts) the named persons are usually the legal owners unless evidence shows special circumstances. Note, a person during life can sell property, make gifts, or transfer things even if they are named in a Will, so <u>people should consider if they already sold or gave away property they also name in a Will gift</u>.

THINGS OWNED IN SPECIAL WAYS MAY LIMIT GIFTING IN WILL

A person should consider if they own real estate or other property in special ways which may limit gifting by Will. Laws in different states vary but <u>some special ways of ownership are</u>:

- "joint tenant with right of survivorship" or similar legal options, so then property transfers automatically to the other named owners regardless of a Will, which in some states is usually how the family house is held (in Kansas often married people do papers so if 1 spouse dies the surviving spouse gets a house).
- papers say a "life estate" exists, so then if life of someone ends the other people in papers get item, and
- "Trust property" if paperwork made a Trust entity and property was actually transferred into it, so then the Trust papers control where things put in the Trust go on someone's death.

"Joint ownership" where many people own a thing can occur if people do joint papers, agree to it, buy with joint funds, or if a gift was to many. Joint property can be gifted by Will, like "I give my half of boat to Ed Hu".

NON-PROBATE TRANSFERS THAT HAPPEN AUTOMATICALLY IGNORE A WILL

Money or property of the deceased that for some reason automatically transfers on death or soon after to new owners is called "non-probate property". Such things transfer as arranged even if Will gifts name the same items. Examples of non-probate property are: a) a "designated beneficiary" form done before names person to get an account or investment, b) transfer-on-death account, and c) real property is held by 2 people as "joint tenants with survivorship" or similar so at a death the surviving person gets things. Property in a Trust usually ignores a Will and transfers as Trust papers say. Life insurance is usually paid to a named beneficiary. Trying to do non-probate transfers for all things is called "avoiding probate", but few people try this since it can cause years of hassle, benefits are small, and often a small thing is missed. <u>When doing a Will a person should consider non-probate transfers that will occur automatically on death and consider what property and money will be left to transfer by Will</u>.

"HELPFUL INFORMATION" FORM CAN TELL FAMILY AND FRIENDS THINGS

Often people do a "Helpful Information" form that some financial planners, lawyers, and banks suggest so family and friends after a death know things. Often people staple records or lists to this. <u>See next pages</u>.

ESTATE PLANNING HELPFUL INFORMATION

<u>For more space attach copies of form or blank pages. Keep pages by Will or other place for Executor or family.</u>

1. Personal Information (Name, Birthdate, Social Security number, special family details, other)**:**

2. Real estate, vehicles, and other major tangible property (especially if people may not find them):

3. Non-tangible assets like stocks, accounts, investments, loans owed you, and business interests:

4. Possible income or insurance like pensions, retirement, disability, insurance, or contracts:

5. Debts owed by you like credit card, loan, student loan, mortgage, car loans, and accounts payable:

6. Names and information of professionals used (attorneys, accountants, brokers, doctors, others):

7. Computer passwords and helpful files, document places, and safes or safe-deposit boxes code/key:

8. Other helpful things, wishes for funeral, special requests, and last messages to family and friends:

CHAPTER 3
WILL BASICS

WILL LETS "TESTATOR" CONTROL THINGS AFTER DEATH

A Will is done by a person to control some things after their death. A person doing a Will is called the "Testator" or "Will maker". A Testator when signing must be at least 18 years old, of sound mind (rational with sufficient memory), and not be under duress (unfair pressure or threat). Most people can do a Will.

SIGN WILL WITH 2 WITNESSES

A WILL IN KANSAS USUALLY MUST BE WRITTEN AND HAVE 2 WITNESSES

To be a valid Will in Kansas usually it must a) show it is meant as a Will, b) be done on paper, and c) be signed with 2 witnesses. In Kansas a "Video Will" or "Audio Will" or similar usually has no legal effect. Unlike some states Kansas doesn't let people skip using 2 witnesses if a Will is all handwritten. Kansas technically may let people about to die do a Will orally by speaking to 2 persons, but then witnesses must put it in writing within 30 days and not benefit from it, it only affects "personal property" so no real property or most financial assets, and this more often causes legal problems so is not recommended. See K.S. 59-608.

WITNESSES SHOULD BE PEOPLE AT LEAST AGE 18

A person to act as a witness must be at least age 18. It is not required but preferable a witness not be old or live far away. Often used as witnesses are neighbors, friends, strangers, and maybe family members.

WITNESSES OFTEN AREN'T GIVEN THINGS IN WILL OR NAMED TO DO THINGS

Kansas does let a person named in Will gifts or similar be a witness. But the law will ignore and not do Will things that benefit a witness unless there are 2 other proper witnesses or unless the witness is close family and would get more under "intestate law" if there were no Will. See K.S. 59-604. To avoid the issue most people use as witnesses people not benefitting from what a Will says. And though not required most people also try to use as witnesses people not named in a Will as Executor, Guardian, or Conservator.

TESTATOR AND 2 WITNESSES SIGN A WILL WHEN TOGETHER IN 1 ROOM

The person doing the Will must sign it with 2 witnesses who then also sign the Will. Everyone should be in 1 room and see all others sign. Witnesses and Testator showing an ID is not required but common. A Testator or witness usually do use their full legal name in a Will unless they dislike it and rarely used it. The Testator need not initial Will pages. The witnesses usually only read the 1 paragraph they sign below. People who can't move a hand to sign should consult a lawyer. A Testator need not verbally tell people it is their Will, but if this is done it is usually called "publishing a Will". Though not required often a Testator says a thing like, "My name is _____ and this is the Will I want and do voluntarily and want people to witness". Some Testators chat with witnesses a few minutes about the Will to show they know what they're doing.

KEEP SIGNED WILL IN SAFE PLACE IT CAN BE FOUND AFTER A DEATH

People should keep a Will so it can be found within days of a death, like in a desk, drawer, safe, or less often safe deposit box. It can be given to a person to hold. It may help to say how to find and get a Will. Kansas unlike some states usually does not let people during their life file a Will at court for safekeeping.

CANCELING OLD WILLS IS USUALLY NOT A PROBLEM

So a new Will is followed old Wills should be canceled ("revoked") but this is easy and rarely a problem. A new Will usually quickly says old Wills are revoked to cancel them, and all this book's Will forms say this. A few people revoke a Will by writing "void" or "cancelled" or "X" on a Will, preferably with a witness to this. Usually crossing out just part of a Will has no effect, and revoking a Will doesn't bring back an earlier Will.

MOST WILLS SAY TO SKIP COSTLY BOND

Most Wills helpfully say no "bond" or "surety" is required for any Executor, Guardian, or similar people. This is insurance bought from an company to insure against misconduct. But the person writing a Will usually doesn't want a bond since the person named is trusted and buying insurance uses up estate assets.

MOST WILLS SAY PEOPLE MAY LATER DO INFORMAL PROBATE

Most Wills say people may later do "informal probate" which can avoid later costs and delays. In informal probate any probate legal process is usually faster and can be done with less cost. Also, if a decedent left under $40,000 of things then simpler legal options can be used to do things in a few months.

IN WILL NAME EXECUTOR TO DO THINGS AFTER A DEATH

WILL NAMES "EXECUTOR" TO ACT AND HAVE POWER AFTER A DEATH

Usually a Will names someone as "Executor" to act after a death like carry out gifts, handle debts, and do probate. The law gives Executors many powers and rights to do things, like collect and move money and property to new owners. If a Will does not name a person a judge can pick someone, but family may argue about who to pick. Naming 2 people to both do this job is possible but rare due to risk of arguments and delay, and since any 1 person named should be trusted. The person named Executor can get Will gifts. Note, in Kansas the term "Personal Representative" is increasingly used in Wills and official legal papers for person handling things after a death. But most people and this book still use the older term of Executor.

EXECUTOR CAN BE PAID AND ESTATE PAYS FOR EXECUTOR'S EXPENSES

An Executor can ask to be paid, and the pay they get is usually seen as fair for their work. An average example of an Executor may be one who over 10 months spends 100 hours of work on an estate with house and property worth $500,000, and maybe $4000 is later paid for Executor's work so under 1% of things. But often Executors often don't ask for pay to not owe income tax and leave more money to carry out Will gifts. Any lawyer hired by Executor is often paid by the hour. Expenses an Executor has like for lawyers, repairs, fees, insurance, monthly mortgage payments, other bills, and other usual things comes from estate assets.

EXECUTOR IS PERSON AT LEAST 18 AND SECOND PERSON RARELY NEEDED

A person to be Executor must be 18 or older. They needn't have a clean criminal record, or be a state resident or U.S. citizen but being local can make later work easier. But a judge may later block or remove a person doing a bad job or who seems very unsuitable like for past big crimes. Some people name a 2nd person to be Executor if the 1st person is unavailable, but most skip this since it's rarely needed, if a problem is seen a new Will can be done, or a judge can pick someone. But if wanted to add such a 2nd person words can be added to a Will, like: "or if they are reasonably unable to serve I name _____ to serve".

CHAPTER 4
WILL GIFTS INCLUDING RESIDUE CLAUSE

MAIN USE OF A WILL IS TO SAY GIFTS TO HAPPEN AFTER DEATH

Most people use a Will to say what happens to their property and money after their death, usually by making various Will gifts. Verbal and even written statements about this are not usually valid if outside a proper Will. A Will can control property acquired after it was signed. The very end of this chapter explains "intestate law" which controls where things go at a person's death if no valid Will handles this.

GIFTING IN A WILL USING SIMPLE WORDS OFTEN IS BEST

Making gifts in a Will using simple words is often best, using words like "I give to" and "I gift to". This is legally fine and avoids confusing legal words like "bequest", "devise", and "legacy" which few people know.

A PERSON IS MOSTLY FREE TO GIFT THEIR THINGS AS WANTED

People are mostly free to give at death their money and property as they want. But a spouse, minor children under age 18, and creditors owed money may have some rights which this book later explains.

IN WILL CAN DO "SPECIFIC GIFTS" TO GIFT PARTICULAR PROPERTY

Most Wills have "specific gifts" to gift <u>particular things</u>. Specific gifts can be any property, like "I give boat to Ed Blom" and "I give UBank account #84553873 to Sue Wu". If a gift is not clear the law assumes all of a kind of thing is given, like "I give jewelry to Ann Po" means <u>all</u> jewelry. But gifting specific property can have surprises like value of an item can change, or a Will gift may fail to occur since property is no longer owned.

IN WILL CAN DO "GENERAL GIFTS" LIKE OF MONEY

Wills can do "general gifts" where what is gifted is not particular property but can be flexibly chosen, like "I give 1 of my 3 cars to Ed Po" which lets an Executor pick which car. The usual general gift is money, like "I give $5 to Ed Vu". Money gifts are easy to write, let equal gifts be made, and are safer since specific items might not be owned at death. To carry out money gifts an Executor uses accounts or sells some property.

"RESIDUE CLAUSE" IS CATCH-ALL THAT HELPFULLY GIFTS ANYTHING LEFT

Most Wills by their end have a Residue Clause to gift property or money not gifted or used in a Will or other way, often called a "catch-all" or "left-over" clause. <u>The Residue Clause is covered later in this Chapter</u>.

CONDITIONS ON WILL GIFTS ARE RARE DUE TO POSSIBLE PROBLEMS

Putting conditions on a gift, like "I give Ann Poe $90 if she graduates college", can cause problems like years of delay, risk of lawsuits, and big attorneys fees, and due to this conditions are rarely put on Will gifts.

PROPERTY OR MONEY IN A "JOINT GIFT" GOES TO MULTIPLE PEOPLE

The same property or money in a "joint gift" can go to multiple people to each get a part interest, like "I give boat and all hats to Ann Wu and Sue Han" means each person owns 50% of every item. People later can split things by agreement or as Executor suggests, or Executor can just sell items and split the money. If a person in a joint gift has died their part of things usually is left to transfer under the Residue Clause.

GIFT BENEFICIARIES CAN GET PERCENTAGE RATHER THAN EQUAL SHARE

If a Will gift goes to multiple people the law assumes equal shares, but if wanted percentages can be used to make unequal gifts, like "I give boat 90% to Ed Wu and 10% to Joe Hud".

LATER DIVORCE OR MURDER CANCELS WILL GIFTS

Kansas law says a person divorcing or murdering Testator usually cancels all Will gifts to the person.

AFTER A DEATH FAMILIES OFTEN LET PEOPLE TAKE ITEMS UNOFFICIALLY

As this book later says Kansas law lets people write a short list or memo to add gifts of certain property to a Will. Also, after a death many families unofficially let people take small items in ways a dead person wrote on notes, put on stickers, mentioned, or would want, and this often isn't a problem unless someone objects. If anyone objects a judge usually will order property and money be handed out as a Will and other legal things say, but afterward people who got things are free to voluntarily hand out things to do what decedent wanted.

CAN LEAVE SOME WILL GIFT LINES BLANK OR WRITE THINGS LIKE "SKIPPED"

A person writing a Will can choose to not use some gifts lines in a Will legal form, like by just leaving them blank, writing things like "SKIPPED" or "NONE" in them, or using a computer to delete some gift lines. Judges and others usually do not care about neatness or empty spaces in Wills.

OPTIONS EXIST TO HANDLE RARE CASE PERSON IN A WILL GIFT DIES

PERSON IN WILL GIFT USUALLY MUST SURVIVE OR GIFT DOES NOT OCCUR

Though rarely an issue, many Wills like this book's Will forms say a person named in a Will gift must survive (live past) the Testator or the gift will not later occur unless gift language specifically says different. If survival isn't required like this then what occurs can be unclear (for many reasons like certain state laws). Most people if they see a person in a gift has died just re-do a Will or trust a Residue Clause to handle it.

SOME PEOPLE ADD "ALTERNATE BENEFICIARY" MAYBE FOR SPECIAL ITEMS

Some people to handle if a person named in a Will gift dies maybe put for special items an alternate beneficiary, like for example: "I give oak table to Ed Wu but if they don't survive me to Ben Fox".

IF PERSON IN WILL GIFT DIES IT CAN GO TO "LINEAL DESCENDANTS"

A Will gift can say it goes to a person but if they don't survive the Testator then say the gift goes to the person's "lineal descendants". Descendants are a person's children and grandchildren. Also, the term "per stirpes" is often used to say to give to each family branch equally. An example shows how this works:

A Will may say: "All clothes to Sue Wu but if they don't survive to their lineal descendants per stirpes", and this means if Sue Wu has died and her son Ken Wu is living and her other son Ben Wu has died but left 2 children then, legally, by law Ken Wu himself gets 50% and Ben Wu's 2 children each get 25%.

HELPFUL LAWS OFTEN REQUIRE PERSON SURVIVE 120 HOURS TO GET GIFT

Laws in most states say a person dying within 120 hours of someone is seen as having died earlier, so often a Will gift to them is ignored. This avoids legal problems like need to know exact time of death and, also, having an item go through many probate legal cases over years.

RESIDUE CLAUSE GIFTING ALL LEFT IS MAIN WAY USED TO GIFT THINGS

THE "RESIDUE CLAUSE" IS CATCH-ALL THAT HELPS GIFT ANYTHING LEFT

Most Wills by their end have a <u>Residue Clause to gift any property or money not gifted earlier in a Will or used in other ways</u>. Things transferred this way is called the "Residue". Many people <u>gift most their money and property this way by intentionally not mentioning in a Will most things so the Residue Clause handles it</u>. Using the Residue Clause to give things avoids need to describe things and has less legal risk. Many people with a spouse or young children mostly use a Residue Clause and don't do many other gifts. After applying a Residue Clause if anything is somehow left then a decedent's closest heirs get things (this is closest family).

USUAL RESIDUE CLAUSE HAS 2 PARTS

A short 2 part Residue Clause is usual and is used in this book's Will forms, and it has:

1) 1st space to name 1 or more persons to get things if they survive Testator (many name a spouse or closest family here), and if several people are named but only some survive then survivors split things, and

2) 2nd space to name persons to get things if all in the 1st space don't survive (many people name next close family or friends in this space), and if a person in 2nd space has died their descendants get their share.

EXAMPLE OF 2 PART RESIDUE CLAUSE:

"RESIDUE CLAUSE: I give money and property not gifted earlier:

A) to _____ my husband John Paul Doe _____ if they survive me, then

B) to _____ Sam Doe my son, Beth Wu my daughter, and Greta Fisher my friend _____ and if any of those just named do not survive me their part goes to their lineal descendants, per stirpes."

In this example if John Paul Doe has survived then he gets all things, but if John Paul Doe hasn't survived and also Sam Doe hasn't survived and he left 2 daughters then those 2 daughters split the 1/3 share of Sam Doe so get 1/6 each and other 2 persons in second part Beth Wu and Greta Fisher get 1/3 each.

PEOPLE CAN PUT SAME THING IN PARTS, OR SKIP PART, OR USE PERCENTAGE

Some people <u>put the same 1 person in both parts</u> of a Residue Clause, to fully ensure that 1 person or if they later die their descendants will get things. Or a person with no spouse <u>may skip the Residue Clause 1st part and in the 2nd part put their children</u> (including any who died who had a child), so all branches of a family get an equal share. *See Appendix.* Many people use <u>percentages in the Residue Clause</u>. *See Appendix.*

SOME PEOPLE CHANGE A RESIDUE CLAUSE TO HAVE 1 PART

Some people change a Residue Clause to have just 1 part since this can gift more equally and be easier to understand. *See example in Appendix.* For example a Residue Clause can be made to say:

"The rest, residue, and remainder of my estate, and anything else, I give to _____ who survive me and if any of those just named do not survive me their part goes to their lineal descendants per stirpes."

MUST SUFFICIENTLY DESCRIBE NAMES AND PROPERTY IN WILL GIFTS

PUTTING NAMES OF PEOPLE OR GROUPS IN WILL GIFTS IS FAIRLY EASY

Putting names in Wills is fairly easy. A judge or Executor assume a person meant people they know so common names are OK unless 2 friends or family use the same name. Details can help if names won't be recognized or to be friendly, like "I give $5 to maid Sue Ax" and "I give $5 to loyal pal Ed Lee". If people mostly used a nickname "also known as" or "a/k/a" may help, like "I give $5 to Dan Smith a/k/a Old Fishy". Gifts can go to a charity, government, or group, like "I give $5 to The Salvation Army, "I give $5 to Johnson County Library, KS", and "I give $5 to Lob Church in Hart, TX". People often phone to get a charity's name.

PUTTING DESCRIPTIONS OF ITEMS IN WILL GIFTS IS FAIRLY EASY

Describing items in gifts is easy since people rarely own similar items, so often fine is "I give ax to Ed Wu" and "I give big table to Ann Fox". It's OK to gift by category or list, for example "I give tools to Sam Lee" and "I give cow, van, and harp to Sue Mo". Financial assets can use plain words, like "bank accounts" or "stocks", but some details can help, like "UBank account ending #1511". Using item location is risky as judges may ignore Will gifts if it seems items were placed to affect gifting and no "independently significant" life reason. So, "I give Ed Po items in safe and desk" a judge may not follow, but "I give Ed Po hats at cabin" likely is OK.

DESCRIBING REAL PROPERTY IS HARD SO MANY USE RESIDUE OR TITLE

The easier and safer way to gift real property (real estate) at death is: 1) do nothing specific so it's handled by a Will Residue Clause, or 2) have a broker or lawyer add names to land title papers to get real property.

Gifting real property other ways is rarely done and hard, though there are ways. Helpfully a Will gift of real property by location does gift all land, buildings, and fixtures there with no need to describe what's there.

Giving real property in a Will using a "legal description" is how some lawyers do it, but this can be hard to do. If using a legal description people must copy without mistakes the full legal description of maybe many lines into a Will. A legal description might be found on a deed or mortgage papers but it must not be abbreviated. Legal descriptions may refer to a "lot" or "blocks" in a subdivision which is recorded in the County Register of Deeds, or it may refer to a path around the land borders with various angles, distances, and iron stakes.

It is possible but less common to gift real property with plain words, like a house by "I give 21 Salem Road, Wichita, Kansas to Mary Ellen Brown".

People can do a blanket gift giving all of a kind of property, like, "I give all real property and fixtures I own in Ford County, KS to Ann Sue Hu" or "I give all real property and fixtures located in any place to Paul Ian Rex".

MOST WILLS HAVE A "MISCELLANEOUS" PART WITH HELPFUL LANGUAGE

Most Wills have a "Miscellaneous" part with paragraphs of legal language to avoid some legal problems.

PERSON BENEFITTING FROM WILL USUALLY SHOULDN'T WRITE OUT A WILL

Kansas law says if a person prepares a Will for someone then things that benefit the person or their parent, child, grandchild, sibling, or spouse might not be done if anyone complains, unless a Testator had other legal advice and knew all the Will said. *See K.S. 59-605.* Helpfully the law does say people can always get up to the amount they'd get if there were no Will under state "intestate law". Due to all this it may be best if a person doesn't prepare a Will or fill in blanks in a legal form if they or their family will benefit from it.

SIMPLE WILL WITH MOST GIFTING DONE BY RESIDUE CLAUSE IS OFTEN BEST

Writing a simple Will without many gifts, much left blank, and mostly using a Residue Clause is often best.

If there is a spouse often a person does small gifts to friends and family, then uses the Residue Clause of the Will to gift all remaining to their spouse, and then names a few fallback persons in the Residue Clause.

If there is no spouse and no child often a person does a few small gifts, and then names some family or friends in the Residue Clause to get everything remaining.

A parent with young children if married to the other parent often does very small gifts to friends and family, then uses the Residue Clause to gift all remaining to their spouse, and then names as fallbacks the young children in the Residue Clause.

A parent with young children if not married or close to the other parent often does very small gifts to friends and family, and then uses the Residue Clause to gift all remaining to their children.

"INTESTATE" LAW SAYS WHERE THINGS GO AT DEATH IF THERE IS NO WILL

State "intestate law" says where a dead person's property and money left goes if there is no valid Will or if anything is left after a Will is followed. Some people like what intestate law says and intentionally skip doing a Will. Intestate law basically gives things to certain closest surviving (living) family a decedent left. Note, by law if a family member is dead a surviving child of them often gets to receive things in their place. Kansas for its intestate law basically says starting at Kansas Statutes 59-504 as follows:

- if spouse survives and no children, the spouse gets all,

- if children survive and no spouse, the children get all,

- if some children and also a spouse survive, the children get 1/2 and the spouse gets 1/2,

- if parents of the decedent survive but no children or spouse, the parents get all,

- if some brothers or sisters survive but no spouse, children, or parents, the brothers and sisters get all, and

- if none of the above named relatives of a decedent survive, then more distant surviving family of decedent get things, and if no such family exist it goes to the State of Kansas (it "escheats", which is very rare).

CHAPTER 5
DEBT, MARRIAGE, AND YOUNG CHILD ISSUES

DEBT ISSUES

PAYING DECEDENT'S DEBTS MAY USE UP RESOURCES AND REDUCE GIFTS

Creditors a decedent owed can ask a judge to be paid from decedent's money and property before Will gifts and other transfers are done. How creditors are paid is set by state law and a Wil need not cover this. Funds to pay creditors comes from decedent's property and estate so may affect (in order) the Will Residue, Will general gifts, Will specific gifts, and then non-probate transfers. Some debts like for probate, attorneys, funeral, and health care may have priority to be paid first. For many reasons often not all creditors are paid. A spouse and family usually aren't usually liable for decedent's debts unless they guaranteed or co-signed. People should consider how paying debts may use up money or property, leaving less to carry out Will gifts.

"FAMILY RIGHTS" MAY BE CLAIMED TO GET FAMILY THINGS EARLY

Most states in laws have "family rights" a decedent's surviving spouse or children under 18 can choose to use or not, and this lets them get some of decedent's things before most of decedent's debts and also before a Will and certain transfers are done. States vary but this can include a "family allowance" right to get from decedent's things support for family often for 1 year or so of probate, and "exempt property" right to claim $30,000 or so of decedent's household items. And if decedent didn't leave a big estate often a "small estate" affidavit or similar can be used and not full probate to get family most things maybe without paying debts. All this can help family if decedent had big debts or help in cases where family feel they didn't get enough. Clearly if a spouse or minor children choose to use family rights this leaves less to carry out a Will and other transfers. Partly so family don't bother to use family rights most people by Will and other ways give mostly to any spouse or children under 18 (like over 50% and any family home). People can research their state's laws.

HOME OFTEN GOES TO FAMILY INCLUDING DUE TO "HOMESTEAD" LAW

Laws in states vary but a house and nearby land a person owns and lives at is often called a "homestead". A person by Will often gifts a homestead to a spouse or their children under 18 living there. Or a person often puts a spouse or young children on the land title as "joint tenant" or similar to get things on the person's death. Importantly, many states have a "homestead law" saying decedent's spouse or children under 18 have a legal right to get the homestead to own or in some states to live at till all children are 18 or a spouse dies. Clearly if family use a homestead law this may block or delay a person trying to give a homestead to others. For many reasons usually a person gives a family house to a spouse or to young children. Other laws mostly protect a house from creditors without a proper mortgage or lien. People can research their state's laws.

SECURED DEBTS LIKE MORTGAGE OR VEHICLE LIEN ARE NOT PAID OFF

Most Wills and Kansas law says usually don't pay off secured debts like a house mortgage or vehicle lien on decedent's property even if other debts are paid off by Executor or in probate. This avoids using a lot of estate resources on paying off large secured debts. But if wanted a Testator can a) gift in Will enough money to pay such debts, or b) put in Will an order to pay (like, "I order the Executor to pay the home mortgage paid off"). Most banks let new owners who got things after a death make the same monthly payments on a secured debt.

MARRIAGE ISSUES

MOST STATES USE "SEPARATE PROPERTY LAW" FOR SPOUSES

Kansas and most states use the "Separate Property Law" system which says married people <u>mostly own all their money and property separately</u> and not jointly with a spouse. Due to this in Kansas a spouse is technically free to sell during life or gift in Will what they wholly own and don't share with their spouse. But joint ownership by 2 spouses can arise in many ways, like by paying half a purchase price, by agreement, if a gift is to both spouses, or if spouses do joint ownership papers. And many married people do land title papers to hold a house a certain way so on a spouse's death it then automatically goes to the other spouse.

"COMMUNITY PROPERTY" LAW APPLIES IN OTHER STATES FOR SPOUSES

There are 9 states mostly in West and South U.S.A. that use "Community Property" law for spouses there (Arizona, California, Louisiana, Idaho, Nevada, New Mexico, Texas, Washington, and Wisconsin). This law says <u>property or money is owned 50/50 by spouses as "Community Property"</u> if it comes from physical or mental effort while living there and married (like labor or wages, management of a business, or active trading of a collection or stocks) or if it was bought or improved with other Community Property. Most people in Kansas avoid these issues unless they recently moved from any of these states.

"JOINT WILL" SIGNED BY BOTH SPOUSES IS NOT RECOMMENDED

Some couples sign 1 "Joint Will" or "Contract To Make A Will" done by a lawyer saying a spouse gives all to the other if they die first, then says last living spouse gives to all children equally, and usually says a spouse may <u>not</u> change this. This is not recommended, banned in some states, and few people do this.

SPOUSE CAN CLAIM "ELECTIVE SHARE" INSTEAD OF THEM FOLLOWING WILL

In Kansas like in many states a spouse <u>if unhappy with what a Will and other transfers may give them</u> does have a <u>legal right to choose (elect) an "Elective Share" of their dead spouse's things</u> rather than take what a Will says they get. This is done for fairness, so a surviving spouse has resources to live on, and so early divorce isn't needed to feel financially secure. The Elective Share starts at 3% at 1 year of marriage, goes up by 3% yearly, and it's 50% after 15 years, and often a spouse can get all of the first $50,000 as a minimum. The law is complex and considers many transfers, deductions, and if overall a spouse was treated fairly. To avoid legal tricks the Elective Share can cover items a spouse recently gifted away or controlled but didn't technically own. And as this book has said a spouse may have rights to some real property of the decedent. Obviously if a spouse uses the Elective Share and other rights to get some of decedent's property and money this may use up much of decedent's property and money and may interfere with other transfers. <u>To avoid a spouse wanting to use the Elective Share and other rights most married people gift by Will and other ways over 1/2 of their things to any spouse (including any family house).</u>

WILL CAN NAME "GUARDIAN" TO CARE FOR CHILD

If a parent dies with a child under 18 any other natural or adopted parent (but not step-parent) then automatically gets control of the child's care including health care, school, and home, unless they are unavailable or proven unfit in court which is rare. But in case it is needed (like if later both parents die) a Will often names a healthy and willing family member or friend to be "Guardian" to care for a child. Some states call this a "Guardian of the Person".

WILL CAN NAME "CONSERVATOR" TO MANAGE A CHILD'S PROPERTY

Since a child until age 18 can't legally manage money or property a Will often names a person to act as "Conservator" to manage the child's property and money. They also say how to use these for a child's costs (like school, living, and health care costs) till usually age 18 when all left goes to the child. Some states call this a "Guardian of the Estate". Judges often do a yearly hearing to review spending. Anyone paying things for a child can ask to be paid back from the child's money and property. Importantly, most Wills at the end also say an Executor may let a "Custodian" they pick manage a young child's property and money, spend it for their benefit, and at 18 give a child anything left. This is allowed by the "Uniform Transfers To Minors Act" law which lets a Custodian do most things a Conservator does but skips most costs, work, and delays.

MOST WILLS NAME 1 PERSON TO CARE FOR CHILD AND THEIR PROPERTY

This book's Will forms and most people in Kansas name the same person to be Guardian of the Person and be Conservator. People can modify a Will to name different people for these 2 jobs if they really want. But naming different people is not usually worth the bother since parents dying is rare, a young child usually gets things only if both parents are dead so a Guardian of the Person will be involved, and a Guardian of the Person if they disagree on spending may be very angry and even try to sue the Conservator.

PERSON TO BE GUARDIAN OR BE CONSERVATOR MUST BE AT LEAST 18

A person must be at least 18 to be a Guardian of the Person or to be Conservator, but a person needn't be a state resident or U.S. citizen or even have a clean criminal record. The choice for this by last living parent usually is followed. Usually being local does makes later work easier. If no Will picks a person for a position or they're unavailable a judge can pick, but family may argue about this. A judge may later block or remove a person who is doing a very bad job or who seems unsuitable like for past extremely bad crimes. Naming 2 people for a position to help a child to act at the same time is rare since the 2 people may argue and any 1 person named should be trusted, but some people do name a married couple in a stable marriage. Some Wills add a 2nd person in case the 1st person is later unavailable, for example like: "or if they are reasonably unable to serve I name ____ to serve"). But many people skip naming an additional person since it's rarely needed, if a problem is seen a Will can be re-done, and a judge always can name a person to act.

PICKING GUARDIANS RARELY MATTERS DESPITE PARENTS WORRYING

A young child having parents die is rare so parents shouldn't worry that much about this. A very large U.S. study of 311,900 people found 72,240 were under 18 and of these 2014 had lost 1 parent (2.78%) and just 97 both parents (just 0.13%), so losing parents is very rare. *Parent Mortality Census SIPP Paper #288.*

CHAPTER 6
BASIC IDEAS ABOUT HEALTH CARE FORMS

SOME BASIC IDEAS HELP PEOPLE UNDERSTAND HEALTH CARE FORMS

Some ideas help people understand health care forms.

■ By law people controls their own health care by telling medical personnel what they want unless they are "incapacitated" by insufficient ability to a) communicate verbally or by notes, b) be rational, or c) be conscious. Most people keep control of their own care till death or till no big treatment options remain, but some people worry they may be incapacitated a long time so want to do health care forms.

■ Legal documents that help control health care are usually called "Advanced Directives".

■ If an adult 18 or older becomes incapacitated the adult's closest family like spouse or adult child usually can make emergency decisions. But later they usually must then rush to a judge to get further power if no legal document gives them more power over health care.

■ In legal documents a person can be named to have control of health care if needed. This person is often called the "Health Care Agent", "Health Care Attorney-in-Fact", "Health Care Advocate", or a similar name.

■ In legal documents people can write medical instructions doctors, family, and other people must obey.

■ Parents even without legal documents mostly have full power over health care of children under age 18, and the only exception is teens have some freedom to pick their own family planning or gender related care.

■ Some married people do documents to give a spouse power over medical care if they are incapacitated. Some adults especially to age 25 do documents to give this power to parents. The young are less often sick.

■ Pain relief like pain drugs or comfort care is still given even if documents say to stop or limit other care.

■ Most people only do 1 legal document about health care that often names someone to control health care if needed and has a spot for basic instructions (this is sometimes called a "Health Care Power of Attorney").

■ For the rare times stopping health care seems more likely to matter (like due to extreme illness or old age):

-- most people do nothing special and trust family or Health Care Agent to wisely decide when to stop care (they can weigh many factors like pain, cost, likely difficulty of treatment, beliefs, and chances of recovery);

-- a few people do a serious document to say to stop most health care if later doctors think an incapacitated person has very bad health and more medical care likely won't help (sometimes this is called a "Living Will";

-- a few people do a serious document to say starting immediately to not give most medical care (often this is called a "Do-Not-Resuscitate" if about resuscitation, or called a "Physician's Order" if about many treatments).

CHAPTER 7
FORM 1: WILL (STANDARD)

FORM 1 IS A STANDARD WILL THAT IS FLEXIBLE AND WITHOUT A GUARDIAN

Form 1 is a standard Will that is flexible and lets person control some things after their death. This form has no part about a Guardian so this form is for a person with no minor child under age 18. The term "Last Will And Testament" is used since in the past a Testament was a document done with a Will.

FORM IS A WILL WITH SEVERAL PARTS

The form starts with places for a person to put their name (a full legal name is best but not required) and current main residence (most put a county but some put a city). A Will is still valid if people later move.

The 1st paragraph, "Gifts", has many spaces to make either specific gifts of particular property or general gifts like of money. People can delete, copy and paste to add more, or leave blank these gift lines.

The 2nd paragraph, "Separate Writings", says to follow any separate writings done apart from the Will that gifts tangible personal property in manner allowed by state law.

The 3rd paragraph, "Residue", has a Residue Clause to say any property and money left after other Will parts and any other transfers is gifted to persons as the Residue Clause directs.

The 4th paragraph, "Administration", has a space to name a "Personal Representative" to handle legal and other matters after a person's death (this basically means the same thing as an Executor).

The 5th paragraph, "Miscellaneous", has paragraphs of legal language to help avoid certain legal issues.

Last is a paragraph for the person doing the Will to sign and write city or county it is signed in, and a paragraph for 2 witnesses to sign and put their addresses.

USUAL RESIDUE CLAUSE HAS 2 PLACES TO NAME PERSONS TO GET THINGS

In a Will "Residue Clause" anything left over after other Will parts is transferred as the clause directs. Many people use a Residue Clause to gift most or even all things. In the Will form's Residue Clause there is:

1) a 1st space to name 1 or more persons to get the Residue, and if any named here have not died before the Will maker then any other persons named here in this 1st space take their share, and

2) a 2nd space to name people to get things if all people named in the 1st space have died, and if any people named in the 2nd space have died their shares go to "lineal descendants" like their children.

Most people name in the 1st space a spouse or closest family or closest friends, and in 2nd space next closest family or friends. This may seem complex but those in the 1st space most often do get things.

TESTATOR AND 2 WITNESSES WHILE TOGETHER SIGN WILL

This Will after being filled out (except bits intentionally left blank) must be signed by the person doing the Will (the "Testator") in front of 2 persons acting as witnesses at least age 18 who then also sign the Will. Testator and witnesses should be in 1 room and see others sign. Usually people try to pick witnesses so no Will gift is going to them, and so no witness is named as Executor, Guardian, or Conservator in the Will. Witnesses usually just read the 1 paragraph they sign. A Testator does not need to initial the Will pages. Though not required often Testator says a thing like, "My name is _____ and this is my Will that I do voluntarily and want you 2 people to witness".

LAST WILL AND TESTAMENT

I, _____, of _____, Kansas, do revoke all prior Wills, Testaments, and Codicils, and do make, publish, and declare this as my Will. I am of sound mind and under no duress or undue influence and acting voluntarily.

1. GIFTS. I give these gifts in this Will, but to get a gift in this section the recipient must survive me except as otherwise stated below.

I give _____ to _____.

I give _____ to _____.

I give _____ to _____.

I give _____ to _____.

I give _____ to _____.

I give _____ to _____.

I give _____ to _____.

I give _____ to _____.

I give _____ to _____.

I give _____ to _____.

I give _____ to _____.

2. SEPARATE WRITINGS. I may do writings separate from this Will to gift tangible personal property as allowed by state law including Kansas Statutes 59-623, and all such writings should be followed. This Will does not revoke any such writings that now exist. A gift in such a writing to a person who does not survive me is canceled and has no effect. Any such writing not found within 90 days of my death is canceled and has no effect.

3. RESIDUE. I give the rest and residue and remainder of my estate, my money and property of any kind and nature, and anything I have an interest in so long as it was not transferred by other Will provisions (all of which is called the "residue"), as follows:

a) to _____ who survive me with persons just named who survive me taking the share of non-survivors, then

b) to _____ and if any of those just named do not survive me their part goes to their lineal descendants per stirpes.

4. ADMINISTRATION. I name and appoint _____
as Personal Representative including for me, my Will, and my estate.

5. MISCELLANEOUS. The following applies to this Will and generally.

My main residence is in Kansas and Kansas law should apply to this Will.

Priority of Will gifts of the same type is based on the order they are written.

In this document no unfilled part is a mistake and residue spaces may be left blank.

The words "give" and "gift" also means a devise, bequest, grant, legacy, or similar.

A gift of property no longer owned by Testator at death shall lapse and be of no effect including no payment of money shall be done in its place, all without ademption.

If a gift or section in this Will reasonably mentions survival in any way then survival is an absolute condition and anti-lapse laws or similar have no effect.

Unless a Will gift specifies otherwise if a Will gift goes to multiple recipients if any do not survive Testator their part to them lapses and instead goes to other surviving recipients.

Failure to make more or any Will gifts or other provisions to or for current children or a current spouse at the time I do this Will is intentional and not a mistake to remedy.

No gift or transfer I made during my life to a person reduces or offsets a Will gift, unless during my life I expressly usually called it a loan or advancement.

Unless another meaning is shown by context use of plural includes the singular and vice versa, and also masculine, feminine, and neuter words are used interchangeably. Unless another meaning is shown "they" means both one person and multiple persons.

Unless a Will specifically says otherwise a) a secured debt including a mortgage or lien shall not be paid off including by a Personal Representative or in probate, b) a recipient of a Will gift of property takes it subject to debts, c) no recipient of a Will gift who later loses property gifted to them to a debtor or who pays to avoid foreclosure or other loss may require the estate or anyone to pay recipient back, do exoneration, or do or pay anything.

I request and authorize any informal, summary, and quick probate or similar action. Any Personal Representative may act independently with no supervision of any court, including independent administration, and without doing any action or filings in court.

I give any Personal Representative a) the fullest authority, powers, and discretion that is allowed by state law, b) authority to lease, sell, mortgage, convey, or retain property including real property in any such manner and time they deem helpful or proper, and c) authority to settle or pay claims or debts at any time they in their sole discretion choose. Any Personal Representative shall also have all powers that may be given or held by law.

Any Personal Representative shall have sole discretion how to balance people's feelings and pick property or divide a gift to carry out a general gift or a gift to multiple persons.

If context permits the terms Personal Representative, Executor, and Administrator are

interchangeable as if all were written, and Conservator is interchangeable with a Guardian of the Estate or of Property. The terms Residue and Residuary also are interchangeable.

The residue includes lapsed or failed gifts, insurance paid to the estate, any inheritances owed, and property I have or had a power of appointment or testamentary disposition over.

Any Personal Representative, Executor, Administrator, Guardian, Conservator, Custodian, and any fiduciary under this Will or otherwise shall qualify and serve without bond, surety, security, surety bond, or similar.

If part of this Will is by law invalid or unenforceable other provisions remain in effect.

Any Personal Representative may at any time transfer money or property of a minor under age 18 to a Custodian to serve under the Kansas Uniform Transfers to Minors Act or a similar law anywhere. Any Personal Representative may select the Custodian including themselves but if they do not I name for this the person named Conservator in this Will.

TESTATOR

IN WITNESS WHEREOF, I, the Testator, publish, declare, and sign this instrument as my Will which I make voluntarily, and I have set my hand and seal on this Will on the _____ day of _____, 20_____.

_____
Signature of Testator

WITNESSES

We, the persons who sign immediately below, do hereby certify and declare as follows:

the document above of which this paragraph is a part at the time and place stated in the document was freely and voluntarily signed and declared by _____, the Testator, to be the Testator's Will, in the presence of both of us;

that at the time of execution by Testator of this document the Testator was according to our best knowledge and belief of sound and disposing mind and memory and under no restraint; and

in the presence of each other and in Testator's presence and at the Testator's request we have now on the document signed our names as witnesses.

Dated at _____, Kansas, on the _____ day of _____, 20___.

_____   _____
Signature of Witness   Address of Witness

_____   _____
Signature of Witness   Address of Witness

CHAPTER 8
FORM 2: WILL (GUARDIAN)

FORM 2 IS BASIC WILL WITH GUARDIAN CLAUSE FOR YOUNG CHILD

Form 2 is a Will with a Guardian part to be used by a person with a minor child under age 18. The term "Last Will And Testament" is used since in the past a Testament was a document done with a Will.

FORM IS A WILL WITH SEVERAL PARTS

The form starts with places for a person to put their name (a full legal name is best but not required) and current main residence (most put a county but some put a city). A Will is still valid if people later move.

The 1st paragraph, "Gifts", has many spaces to make either specific gifts of particular property or general gifts like of money. People can delete, copy and paste to add more, or leave blank these gift lines.

The 2nd paragraph, "Separate Writings", says to follow any separate writings done apart from the Will that gifts tangible personal property in manner allowed by state law.

The 3rd paragraph, "Residue", has a Residue Clause to say any property and money left after other Will parts and any other transfers is gifted to persons as the Residue Clause directs.

The 4th paragraph, "Administration", has a space to name a "Personal Representative" to handle legal and other matters after a person's death (this basically means the same thing as an Executor).

The 5th paragraph, "Guardian", names a person to if needed care for minor children as Guardian of the Person (like if no parent is available later), and also a "Conservator" to manage their property and money.

The 6th paragraph, "Miscellaneous", has paragraphs of legal language to help avoid certain legal issues.

Last is a paragraph for the person doing the Will to sign and write city or county it is signed in, and a paragraph for 2 witnesses to sign and put their addresses.

USUAL RESIDUE CLAUSE HAS 2 PLACES TO NAME PERSONS TO GET THINGS

In a Will "Residue Clause" anything left over after other Will parts is transferred as the clause directs. Many people use a Residue Clause to gift most or even all things. In the Will form's Residue Clause there is:

1) a 1st space to name 1 or more persons to get the Residue, and if any named here have not died before the Will maker then any other persons named here in this 1st space take their share, and

2) a 2nd space to name people to get things if all people named in the 1st space have died, and if any people named in the 2nd space have died their shares go to "lineal descendants" like their children.

Most people name in the 1st space a spouse or closest family or closest friends, and in 2nd space next closest family or friends. This may seem complex but those in the 1st space most often do get things.

TESTATOR AND 2 WITNESSES WHILE TOGETHER SIGN WILL

This Will after being filled out (except bits intentionally left blank) must be signed by the person doing the Will (the "Testator") in front of 2 persons acting as witnesses at least age 18 who then also sign the Will. Testator and witnesses should be in 1 room and see others sign. Usually people try to pick witnesses so no Will gift is going to them, and so no witness is named as Executor, Guardian, or Conservator in the Will. Witnesses usually just read the 1 paragraph they sign. Though not required often Testator says a thing like, "My name is _____ and this is my Will that I do voluntarily and want you 2 people to witness".

23

LAST WILL AND TESTAMENT

I, _____, of _____, Kansas, do revoke all prior Wills, Testaments, and Codicils, and do make, publish, and declare this as my Will. I am of sound mind and under no duress or undue influence and acting voluntarily.

1. GIFTS. I give these gifts in this Will, but to get a gift in this section the recipient must survive me except as otherwise stated below.

I give _____ to _____.

I give _____ to _____.

I give _____ to _____.

I give _____ to _____.

I give _____ to _____.

I give _____ to _____.

I give _____ to _____.

I give _____ to _____.

I give _____ to _____.

2. SEPARATE WRITINGS. I may do writings separate from this Will to gift tangible personal property as allowed by state law including Kansas Statutes 59-623, and all such writings should be followed. This Will does not revoke any such writings that now exist. A gift in such a writing to a person who does not survive me is canceled and has no effect. Any such writing not found within 90 days of my death is canceled and has no effect.

3. RESIDUE. I give the rest and residue and remainder of my estate, my money and property of any kind and nature, and anything I have an interest in so long as it was not transferred by other Will provisions (all of which is called the "residue"), as follows:
   a) to _____ who survive me with persons just named who survive me taking the share of non-survivors, then
   b) to _____ and if any of those just named do not survive me their part goes to their lineal descendants per stirpes.

4. ADMINISTRATION. I name and appoint _____ as Personal Representative including for me, my Will, and my estate.

5. GUARDIAN. I name and appoint _____ as Guardian of any minor child of mine including if needed to have care, authority, and custody of them. I also name and appoint this same person as Conservator for any minor child and the minor child's property, money, and estate.

6. MISCELLANEOUS. The following applies to this Will and generally.

My main residence is in Kansas and Kansas law should apply to this Will.

Priority of Will gifts of the same type is based on the order they are written.

In this document no unfilled part is a mistake and residue spaces may be left blank.

The words "give" and "gift" also means a devise, bequest, grant, legacy, or similar.

A gift of property no longer owned by Testator at death shall lapse and be of no effect including no payment of money shall be done in its place, all without ademption.

If a gift or section in this Will reasonably mentions survival in any way then survival is an absolute condition and anti-lapse laws or similar have no effect.

Unless a Will gift specifies otherwise if a Will gift goes to multiple recipients if any do not survive Testator their part to them lapses and instead goes to other surviving recipients.

Failure to make more or any Will gifts or other provisions to or for current children or a current spouse at the time I do this Will is intentional and not a mistake to remedy.

No gift or transfer I made during my life to a person reduces or offsets a Will gift, unless during my life I expressly usually called it a loan or advancement.

Unless another meaning is shown by context use of plural includes the singular and vice versa, and also masculine, feminine, and neuter words are used interchangeably. Unless another meaning is shown "they" means both one person and multiple persons.

Unless a Will specifically says otherwise a) a secured debt including a mortgage or lien shall not be paid off including by a Personal Representative or in probate, b) a recipient of a Will gift of property takes it subject to debts, c) no recipient of a Will gift who later loses property gifted to them to a debtor or who pays to avoid foreclosure or other loss may require the estate or anyone to pay recipient back, do exoneration, or do or pay anything.

I request and authorize any informal, summary, and quick probate or similar action. Any Personal Representative may act independently with no supervision of any court, including independent administration, and without doing any action or filings in court.

I give any Personal Representative a) the fullest authority, powers, and discretion that is allowed by state law, b) authority to lease, sell, mortgage, convey, or retain property including real property in any such manner and time they deem helpful or proper, and c) authority to settle or pay claims or debts at any time they in their sole discretion choose. Any Personal Representative shall also have all powers that may be given or held by law.

Any Personal Representative shall have sole discretion how to balance people's feelings and pick property or divide a gift to carry out a general gift or a gift to multiple persons.

If context permits the terms Personal Representative, Executor, and Administrator are interchangeable as if all were written, and Conservator is interchangeable with a Guardian of the Estate or of Property. The terms Residue and Residuary also are interchangeable.

The residue includes lapsed or failed gifts, insurance paid to the estate, any inheritances owed, and property I have or had a power of appointment or testamentary disposition over.

Any Personal Representative, Executor, Administrator, Guardian, Conservator, Custodian, and any fiduciary under this Will or otherwise shall qualify and serve without bond, surety, security, surety bond, or similar.

If part of this Will is by law invalid or unenforceable other provisions remain in effect.

Any Personal Representative may at any time transfer money or property of a minor under age 18 to a Custodian to serve under the Kansas Uniform Transfers to Minors Act or a similar law anywhere. Any Personal Representative may select the Custodian including themselves but if they do not I name for this the person named Conservator in this Will.

TESTATOR

IN WITNESS WHEREOF, I, the Testator, publish, declare, and sign this instrument as my Will which I make voluntarily, and I have set my hand and seal on this Will on the _____ day of _____, 20_____.

_____
Signature of Testator

WITNESSES

We, the persons who sign immediately below, do hereby certify and declare as follows:

the document above of which this paragraph is a part at the time and place stated in the document was freely and voluntarily signed and declared by _____, the Testator, to be the Testator's Will, in the presence of both of us;

that at the time of execution by Testator of this document the Testator was according to our best knowledge and belief of sound and disposing mind and memory and under no restraint; and

in the presence of each other and in Testator's presence and at the Testator's request we have now on the document signed our names as witnesses.

Dated at _____, Kansas, on the ____ day of _____, 20_____.

_____   _____
Signature of Witness   Address of Witness

_____   _____
Signature of Witness   Address of Witness

CHAPTER 9
FORM 3: SELF-PROVING AFFIDAVIT

FORM IS SOMETIMES DONE WITH WILL TO REDUCE LATER LEGAL WORK

This form can be done to help with the later legal work involved with using a Will after a death. This form must be done with a notary. This book's form is the statutory found at Kansas Statutes 59-606.

FORM HELPS TO LATER SHOW WILL WAS PROPERLY SIGNED

This form helps after a death when trying to use a Will to prove it was properly signed. If a Self-Proving Affidavit form is not done more work may be needed later, like later a witness to the Will must say in court or submit a writing about how the Will was signed (or if this is not available other proof may be needed). If this form is not done there is more risk a Will is not followed later. Of people doing Wills about half skip doing a Self-Proving Affidavit mostly due to the hassle of using a notary each time a Will is done, and since it mostly just saves later minor work of people who are probably happy to do work to get things using a Will. Some other states have no Self-Proving Affidavit for Wills and manage fine without it.

FORM IS DONE BY TESTATOR AND 2 WITNESSES SIGNING WITH A NOTARY

To complete the Self-Proving Affidavit form a notary (also called "notary public") must see the form signed by the Testator and 2 witnesses to the Will signing, and then the notary signs and notarizes it. The form is often done a few minutes after a Will is signed but it also can be done much later (even years later) when Testator and 2 witnesses can meet a notary. Any Kansas notary will know how to fill out and sign the Self-Proving Affidavit. The word "respectively" used in the form means "in the order just stated". The Self-Proving Affidavit is usually stapled or paper-clipped to the Will.

SELF-PROVING AFFIDAVIT

State of Kansas   )
) ss.

County of _____)

Before me, the undersigned authority, on this day personally appeared _____,

_____, and _____, known to me to be the Testator and

the witnesses, respectively, whose names are subscribed to the annexed or foregoing instrument in

their respective capacities, and, all of such persons being by me first duly sworn, such

_____, Testator, declared to me and to the witnesses in my presence that such

instrument is the Testator's Will, and that the Testator had willingly made and executed it as the

Testator's free and voluntary act and deed for the purposes therein expressed. Such witnesses,

each on the witness' oath stated to me, in the presence and hearing of the Testator, that the

Testator had declared to them that such instrument is the Testator's Will, and that the Testator

executed same as such and wanted each witness to sign it as a witness. Upon their oaths each

witness stated further that they did sign the will as witnesses in the presence of each other and in

the presence of the Testator and at the Testator's request, and that the Testator at that time

possessed the rights of majority, was of sound mind, and under no restraint.

_____

Testator's Signature

_____   _____

Witness Signature   Witness Signature

Subscribed, acknowledged and sworn to before me by _____, Testator,

and _____ and _____, witnesses, this

_____ day of _____, 20_____.

(seal, if any)

Signed:_____

Official Capacity of Officer:_____

CHAPTER 10
FORM 4: TANGIBLE PERSONAL PROPERTY LIST

FORM LETS GIFTS OF SOME PROPERTY BE EASILY MADE OUTSIDE A WILL

This form lets people easily add to a Will some gifts of property they want to occur after their death. This form is often called by people a "Memorandum", a "Gift List", or often just a "List".

FORM GIVES EASY QUICK WAY TO WRITE MORE GIFTS

This form lets a person easily write more gifts of certain property to occur after their death without having to re-do a Will. To use this form Kansas law requires a valid Will says that Lists can be used, and all this book's Will forms say this. If a List and a Will gift the same item then by law the Will is followed. If multiple Lists gift the same item the more recently done page controls. People can modify an existing List page if they then write a new date and signature. But many people prefer to write out everything all at once so it all has to same date to reduce chances of later confusion. To try to avoid later delay this book's form says a List not found within 90 days of a death will be ignored.

It may help understanding to show the Kansas law allowing Lists, Kansas Statutes 59-623, which says:

"Reference in will to statement to dispose of certain tangible personal property; admissibility.

A will may refer to a written statement or list to dispose of items of tangible personal property not otherwise specifically disposed of by the will, other than money, evidences of debt, documents of title, securities, and properties used in trade or business.

To be admissible under this section as evidence of intended disposition, the writing either must be in the handwriting of the testator or be signed by the testator, and must describe the items with reasonable certainty.

The writing may be referred to as one to be in existence at the time of the testator's death; it may be prepared before or after the execution of the will; and it may be altered by the testator after preparation."

FORM CAN ONLY GIFT "TANGIBLE PERSONAL PROPERTY"

By law the form can only gift "tangible personal property", so only tangible (touchable) things, and not most accounts or investments where ownership is tied to papers, accounts, or an entity like a company. The form can't gift real property (land or buildings), coin or paper money even if they're antiques, or items used in a trade or business. Improper property in a List is ignored. Most people use a List to gift clothes, furniture, cars, boats, materials, things used in a hobby, electronics, appliances, antiques, art, and jewelry.

TO COMPLETE A GIFT LIST A PERSON JUST SIGNS AND DATES IT

A List form to be valid just must be signed by the person who is doing it. Putting a date is not required but standard. Once completed any List form pages are often kept with a Will. To cancel a List it can be thrown away or destroyed or just crossed out.

TANGIBLE PERSONAL PROPERTY LIST

In this writing are gifts of tangible personal property to occur after my death, but this writing if not found by someone within 90 days of my death is canceled.

I may do multiple pages of these writings which should all be seen as a single document with the more recently done page controlling if any gifts conflict.

If a person getting a gift below does not survive me such gift is void and canceled.

PROPERTY ITEMS   **NAMES OF RECIPIENTS**

_____ to _____

_____ to _____

_____ to _____

_____ to _____

_____ to _____

_____ to _____

_____ to _____

_____ to _____

_____ to _____

_____ to _____

_____ to _____

_____ to _____

_____ to _____

_____ to _____

_____ to _____

_____ to _____

_____ to _____

DATE:_____   SIGNED:_____

CHAPTER 11
FORM 5: DURABLE POWER OF ATTORNEY FOR HEALTH CARE DECISIONS

FORM LETS AGENT AND INSTRUCTIONS BE WRITTEN ABOUT HEALTH CARE

This form lets people name an Agent and give instructions to help control health care if later needed. This book's form is largely copied from the statutory form found in law at Kansas Statutes 58-632, but it has small changes to be more clear. This is often the only Estate Planning form on health care people do.

FORM CAN NAME "AGENT" FOR HEALTH CARE AND GIVE INSTRUCTIONS

The form lets someone be named as "Agent" to control health care if later the person doing the form is incapacitated. Often named Agent is a spouse, adult child, relative, or friend. Naming a family member as Agent can avoid their need to rush to see a judge for more power. Workers at a place giving health care usually shouldn't be Agent unless they're a relative. Though rarely needed and rarely done a form can be modified to name additional "alternate" persons to act if the first named person doesn't, like by writing: "If the person named to be agent is unavailable then this person shall serve as agent in their place:_____". The form also has areas for instructions about what to do and not do, but many people skip saying much since they trust the Agent and if health care instructions aren't clear this can cause delay or legal problems.

CAN SAY AGENT ALSO SHOULD CONTROL FUNERAL INSTEAD OF FAMILY

A person can modify the form to say instead of closest family like usual the Agent in the form is in charge of bodily remains including funeral, cremation, and burial issues. For example people could add a thing like: "My Agent named here shall control my bodily remains and related issues like funeral, burial, or cremation". But this is rarely done and most people trust family to control this. Under the law everyone should do things a person wanted done with their body if the estate can afford it especially if arrangements have been made. In Kansas about a third of people pick cremation. Many people also pick "Direct Burial/Cremation" which quickly does burial or cremation without family watching but saves about 3/4ths of the usual costs.

PERSON SIGNS FORM IN FRONT OF EITHER NOTARY OR 2 WITNESSES

The form must be signed in front of either a person who is a notary who then notarizes it, or 2 witnesses at least age 18 who then sign. A person doing the form can't use as a witness someone related to them by blood or marriage or adoption, entitled to part of their estate, financially responsible for their health care, or a person named Agent in the form. Often witnesses are friends, distant family, some health care workers, or strangers. Once done the form usually is shown to places that may give care to put in a person's medical file to follow To cancel the form a person should tell Agent and usually places that saw the form.

OPTIONAL WALLET CARDS CAN BE KEPT NEAR A PERSON

At end of this Chapter is an optional "Wallet Card" form people can keep near them, like in a wallet, in a purse, on a refrigerator, or on a bedside table. This can help health care personnel more quickly learn what legal documents a person has done so they can more quickly find these to read and follow them.

DURABLE POWER OF ATTORNEY FOR HEALTH CARE DECISIONS

GENERAL STATEMENT OF AUTHORITY GRANTED

K.S.A. 58-632

I, _____ , _____ , _____ , designate and appoint:
　　　　　　　　name　　　　　　　　　　date of birth (optional)　　last four digits of SSN (optional)

Name of Agent _____

Address _____

Telephone Number_____

to be my agent for health care decisions and pursuant to the language stated below, on my behalf to:

(1) Consent, refuse consent, or withdraw consent to any care, treatment, service or procedure to maintain, diagnose or treat a physical or mental condition, and to make decisions about organ donation, autopsy and disposition of the body;

(2) make all necessary arrangements at any hospital, psychiatric hospital or psychiatric treatment facility, hospice, nursing home or similar institution; to employ or discharge health care personnel to include physicians, psychiatrists, psychologists, dentists, nurses, therapists or any other person who is licensed, certified or otherwise authorized or permitted by the laws of this state to administer health care as the agent shall deem necessary for my physical, mental and emotional well-being; and

(3) request, receive and review any information, verbal or written, regarding my personal affairs or physical or mental health including medical and hospital records and to execute any releases of other documents that may be required in order to obtain such information.

In exercising the grant of authority set forth above my agent for health care decisions shall:

_____

_____

_____

(Here insert any special instructions or statement of the principal's desires to be followed by the agent in exercising the authority granted).

LIMITATIONS OF AUTHORITY

(1) The powers of the agent herein shall be limited to the extent set out in writing in this durable power of attorney for health care decisions, and shall not include the power to revoke or invalidate any previously existing declaration made in accordance with the Natural Death Act (i.e. Living Will).

(2) The agent shall be prohibited from authorizing consent for the following items:

_____

_____

_____

(3) This durable power of attorney for health care decisions shall be subject to the additional following limitations:

_____

_____

_____

EFFECTIVE TIME

This durable power of attorney for healthcare decisions shall become effective immediately and shall not be affected by my subsequent disability or incapacity or upon the occurrence of my disability or incapacity.

REVOCATION

By execution of this durable power of attorney for healthcare decisions, I revoke any prior durable power of attorney for healthcare decisions, but I do not revoke other powers of attorney, if any, which I have given concerning matters other than healthcare decisions.

I reserve the right to revoke this durable power of attorney for healthcare decisions by an instrument in writing signed by me and either (1) witnessed by two individuals meeting the same qualifications as set forth below, or (2) acknowledged by a notary public.

EXECUTION

Executed this_____ (date), at_____ (city), Kansas.

Principal's Signature_____

This document must be: (1) Witnessed by two individuals of lawful age who are not the agent, not related to the principal by blood, marriage or adoption, not entitled to any portion of principal's estate and not financially responsible for principal's health care; OR (2) acknowledged by a notary public.

Witness Signature _____   Witness Signature _____

Address _____   Address _____

_____   _____

(OR)

STATE OF KANSAS   )
COUNTY OF _____) SS.

This instrument was acknowledged before me on _____ by _____.
                                                     Date   Name of person

_____
        Signature of notary public

(Seal, if any)   My appointment expires: _____

- - OPTIONAL HANDMADE WALLET CARD - -

(this optional form can be kept near a person like in a wallet or purse, on a refrigerator, or on a bedside table to help health care personal more quickly find health care legal documents to read and follow).

ATTN: KANSAS HEALTH CARE PROVIDERS

Name:_____

I have the following Advanced Directives:

_____ **Durable Power of Attorney For Health Care Decisions**

_____ **Living Will Declaration**

_____ **Do Not Resuscitate**

For information contact this person:

_____

(Name and Phone Number)

ATTN: KANSAS HEALTH CARE PROVIDERS

Name:_____

I have the following Advanced Directives:

_____ **Durable Power of Attorney For Health Care Decisions**

_____ **Living Will Declaration**

_____ **Do Not Resuscitate**

For information contact this person:

_____

(Name and Phone Number)

ATTN: KANSAS HEALTH CARE PROVIDERS

Name:_____

I have the following Advanced Directives:

_____ **Durable Power of Attorney For Health Care Decisions**

_____ **Living Will Declaration**

_____ **Do Not Resuscitate**

For information contact this person:

_____

(Name and Phone Number)

ATTN: KANSAS HEALTH CARE PROVIDERS

Name:_____

I have the following Advanced Directives:

_____ **Durable Power of Attorney For Health Care Decisions**

_____ **Living Will Declaration**

_____ **Do Not Resuscitate**

For information contact this person:

_____

(Name and Phone Number)

CHAPTER 12
FORM 6: LIVING WILL DECLARATION

IN FORM CAN SAY TO STOP CARE IF LATER DOCTORS THINK IT WON'T HELP

This form lets a person do serious act of saying stop health care if later doctors think it likely won't help. This long form is mostly used in hospitals or similar places. This book's form is taken almost exactly from the statutory form found in law at Kansas Statutes 65-28, 103.

FORM SAYS STOP CARE IF LATER DOCTORS SAY IT LIKELY WON'T HELP

This form does the serious act of saying stop health care if doctors later think more care won't help. Kansas law is strict and says this form can only stop care if later 2 doctors think a person later has a "terminal condition" (this means they'll likely die within 6 months even if life-sustaining care is given). If a person has done the form, is later incapacitated, and doctors say the condition is terminal, then the form is followed which says:

> "I direct that such [life-sustaining] procedures be withheld or withdrawn, and that I be permitted to die naturally with only the administration of medication or performance of any medical procedure deemed necessary to provide me with comfort care."

A fully healthy person can do the form just in case they later fall ill. But most people skip doing this form since it rarely matters, it is stressful to do, and they trust their family and others to act wisely if a person is ever incapacitated and the issue of stopping care arises.

PERSON SIGNS FORM IN FRONT OF EITHER A NOTARY OR 2 WITNESSES

The form must be signed in front of either a person who is a notary who then notarizes the form, or 2 witnesses at least age 18 who then sign. A person doing the form can't use as a witness someone related to them by blood or marriage or adoption, entitled to part of their estate, financially responsible for their health care, or named to be Agent in the form. Once done the form usually is shown to places that may give care to put in a person's medical file to follow To cancel the form a person usually tells their doctor and any places that saw the form.

LIVING WILL DECLARATION

K.S.A. 65-28, 103

Declaration made this _____ day of _____ (month, year). I, _____,
being of sound mind, willfully and voluntarily make known my desire that my dying shall not be artificially
prolonged under the circumstances set forth below, do hereby declare:

If at any time I should have an incurable injury, disease, or illness certified to be a terminal condition by two
physicians who have personally examined me, one of whom shall be my attending physician, and the physicians
have determined that my death will occur whether or not life-sustaining procedures are utilized and where the
application of life-sustaining procedures would serve only to artificially prolong the dying process, I direct that
such procedures be withheld or withdrawn, and that I be permitted to die naturally with only the administration of
medication or the performance of any medical procedure deemed necessary to provide me with comfort care.

In the absence of my ability to give directions regarding the use of such life-sustaining procedures, it is my
intention that this declaration shall be honored by my family and physician(s) as the final expression of my legal
right to refuse medical or surgical treatment and accept the consequences from such refusal.

I understand the meaning of this declaration and am emotionally and mentally competent to make this declaration.

Signed _____

City, County and State of Residence _____

Date of Birth (optional) _____

Last four digits of SSN (optional) _____

The declarant has been personally known to me and I believe the declarant to be of sound mind. I did not sign the
declarant's signature above for or at the direction of the declarant. I am not related to the declarant by blood or
marriage, entitled to any portion of the estate of the declarant according to the laws of intestate succession or
under any will of declarant or codicil thereto, or directly financially responsible for declarant's medical care.

Witness Signature_____   Witness Signature_____

(OR)

STATE OF KANSAS   )
COUNTY OF _____) SS.

This instrument was acknowledged before me on _____ by _____.
                                                                Date   Name of person

_____
            Signature of notary public

(Seal, if any)   My appointment expires: _____

CHAPTER 13
FORM 7: PRE-HOSPITAL DO NOT RESUSCITATE REQUEST

FORM LETS PERSON SAY TO IMMEDIATELY NO LONGER TRY RESUSCITATION

This form is usually just called the "Do Not Resuscitate" form or just a "DNR" form. This form lets a person do the serious act of saying <u>from now on</u> don't try to resuscitate a person. The form is short so it can be read fast like by paramedics outside hospitals or similar places, but it can be used inside places too. This book's form is taken almost exactly from the statutory form found in law at Kansas Statutes 65-4942 but many hospitals have their own form often on colored paper.

FORM SAYS TO IMMEDIATELY NO LONGER TRY RESUSCITATION LIKE C.P.R.

In the form a person can say <u>starting immediately from now on</u> no longer try <u>resuscitation</u> to restart or help the heart or breathing. Mostly this means cardio-pulmonary resuscitation (C.P.R.) won't be tried (this is forcing air into the mouth and chest compressions) and also electric shocks to the heart won't be tried. <u>This form is rarely done</u> and usually only people with a terminal condition or similar very bad health do it. A doctor or similar professional must sign the form and they can explain when this form should be used. Note, instead of this form the similar "Transportable Physician Orders for Patient Preferences" form is increasingly being used by Kansas since it covers more than just resuscitation (other states call this a POLST, MOLST, or similar names).

FORM IS SIGNED BY A DOCTOR AND PERSON DOING THE FORM

The form must be signed by a doctor or similar health professional, and by person doing the form or someone with authority for them. Once done the form is usually shown to places that may give care to make it part of a person's medical file. Some people keeps copies handy to show paramedics or other people who may want to give health care. A copy of the form might be kept on a bedside table, on home refrigerator, pinned to shirt, in a pocket, or some people wear a D.N.R. bracelet or medallion their doctor can explain. A person while still thinking fine can cancel things like by saying this to doctors or not letting paramedics know about the D.N.R. To cancel the form a person usually tells all places that saw the form.

PRE-HOSPITAL DNR REQUEST FORM

AN ADVANCED REQUEST TO LIMIT THE SCOPE OF EMERGENCY MEDICAL CARE
K.S.A. 65-4942

I,_____, _____, _____, request limited emergency care as herein described:

           name   date of birth   last four digits of SSN
                                   (optional)   (optional)

I understand DNR means that if my heart stops beating or if I stop breathing, no medical procedure to restart breathing or heart functioning will be instituted.

I understand this decision will not prevent me from obtaining other emergency medical care by pre-hospital care providers or medical care directed by a physician prior to my death.

I understand I may revoke this directive at any time.

I give my permission for this information to be given to the pre-hospital care providers, doctors, nurses, or other health care personnel as necessary to implement this directive.

I hereby agree to the "Do Not Resuscitate" (DNR) directive

Signature_____   Date_____

Witness Signature_____   Date_____

I AFFIRM THIS DIRECTIVE IS THE EXPRESSED WISH OF THE PATIENT, IS MEDICALLY APPROPRIATE, AND IS DOCUMENTED IN THE PATIENT'S PERMANENT MEDICAL RECORD.

In the event of an acute cardiac or respiratory arrest, no cardiopulmonary resuscitation will be initiated.

Attending Physician Signature_____   Date_____

Address_____   Facility or Agency Name_____

* Signature of physician not required if the above-named is a member of a church or religion which, in lieu of medical care and treatment, provides treatment by spiritual means through prayer alone and care consistent therewith in accordance with the tenets and practices of such church or religion.

REVOCATION PROVISION

I hereby revoke the above declaration.

Signature_____   Date_____

CHAPTER 14
FORM 8: GENERAL DURABLE POWER OF ATTORNEY

FORM LETS POWER BE GIVEN OVER PROPERTY, MONEY, AND MORE

This form lets a person give power to someone to do things with a person's property, money, and more. This book's form is a standard form by the Kansas Judicial Council group of judges and lawyers to provide a standard form for Kansas. Note, the form is called "durable" since it uses the more common option of saying it still has power if the person who did the form is later incapacitated but alive. Note, the form is effective immediately once signed which is now standard and it doesn't use the old option of a "springing power of attorney" which only has power once an event can be proven (such as a person has fallen ill).

FORM GIVES POWER TO LET SOMEONE DO THINGS

This form lets a person give power to someone trusted like a spouse, adult child, or friend over their money, property, records, and other things. The person giving power is called "Principal" and person getting power called "Attorney in Fact" (sometimes called the "Agent"). This form can let someone help do things like pay bills, use accounts, buy or sell items, sign contracts, hire workers, take out debt, and get records. The form may help if person is sick or busy, and may avoid having to use more serious legal options like a guardianship involving a court. A person who isn't incapacitated can overrule or fire the Attorney in Fact.

FORM GIVES NORMAL POWERS AND CAN INITIAL TO GIVE RARER POWERS

The form gives most normal powers to let an Attorney in Fact do most things people want, like move money around, pay bills, get records, and hire workers. Some powers are seen as rarely needed and more dangerous so by law aren't considered given unless initials are put in the "Optional Powers" part of the form. If a person wants the Attorney in Fact to have to keep and show extensive records the "Accounting" area of the form can be marked.

DUE TO RISKS MANY SKIP FORM OR CONSULT A LAWYER

Many people skip this form or first see a lawyer. Using this form is risky and can lead to harm since the Attorney in Fact can be wasteful with money, commit fraud or theft, or by carelessness allow other harms. A person acting as Attorney in Fact has a duty to be loyal and act reasonably and can be sued, but they may be out of money to pay. Usually banks and others can't be blamed for obeying an Attorney in Fact. The law is complex and basic acts may be fine like paying bills but some acts may be improper like making gifts, risky investments, or unusual acts. It is best if a person not their Attorney in Fact does unusual things.

PERSON SIGNS FORM IN FRONT OF A NOTARY

A person should sign the form in front of a notary who then notarizes it. Once it is done some very cautious people quickly show the form to banks and similar places to say they should follow the form later. When an Attorney in Fact signs anything it should be like, for example: "Ed Hu signing as Attorney in Fact under a Power of Attorney for Ann Wu". To cancel the form a person should tell the Attorney in Fact and take back all copies and maybe also tell places that saw the form. It is optional but some people have the Attorney in Fact do the "Acceptance" page, and later some banks have them sign the "Certification" page.

GENERAL DURABLE POWER OF ATTORNEY

(Kansas Judicial Council Form)

(1) I, _____ (principal), of
_____ (street address),
appoint _____ (attorney in fact) of
_____ (street address) as my
attorney in fact under the Kansas Power of Attorney Act, K.S.A. 58-650 to K.S.A. 58-665.
In the event of the subsequent disability, death or disqualification of the attorney in fact I have
designated, I appoint _____ (name) of
_____ (street address).

(2) This is a durable power of attorney and the authority of my attorney in fact shall not terminate if I become disabled or in the event of later uncertainty as to whether I am dead or alive.

(3) This durable power of attorney shall become effective immediately.

GENERAL GRANT OF AUTHORITY

(4) General powers are granted to my attorney in fact and my attorney in fact is granted the power to act with respect to all lawful subjects and purposes and my attorney in fact's authority shall extend to and include each and every action or power which an adult who is not disabled may carry out through an agent specifically authorized in the premises, with respect to any and all matters whatsoever, except as provided in paragraph (7).

(5) The general authority granted and assumed by the attorney in fact shall include, but not be limited to the following acts, conducted either directly or by electronic means:

(a) To ask, demand, sue for, recover, collect and receive any and all such sums of money, debts, deposits, certificates of deposit, accounts, legacies, bequests, interest dividends, annuities, and demands whatsoever as now or shall hereafter become due, owing payable or belonging to me, including any proceedings under the Bankruptcy Act or similar statutes;

(b) To write checks on any of my checking accounts, deposit and withdraw moneys from savings accounts, sign or endorse checks of any nature payable to me, assign or transfer stock certificates, and certificates of deposit and enter any safety deposit box leased in my name or my name and others if I would otherwise be permitted access to such box;

(c) To maintain, repair, improve, manage, insure, rent, lease, sell, convey, mortgage, in any way or manner deal with all or any part of any real or personal property whatsoever, tangible or intangible, or any interest, including joint interest in such property, that I now own or may later acquire, for me, on my behalf, in my name and under such terms and conditions and such other covenants as my attorney in fact may deem proper and in my name to make, execute, acknowledge good and sufficient deeds of conveyance or other instrument or instruments necessary to effect such sale, conveyance or agreement;

(d) To conduct, engage in, and transact any and all lawful business of whatsoever nature or kind for me, on my behalf, and in my name. including exercising any rights I may hold as an owner of an interest in a business entity or sole proprietorship;

(e) To transfer any interests in property I may own to a revocable or living trust created by me, which trust benefits me during my life;

(f) To participate or not participate, as my attorney in fact may determine, in any program, plan or activity dealing with agricultural land or practices sponsored by or under the supervision or direction of the United States Department of Agriculture (USDA), Farm Service Agency (FSA), Commodity Credit Corporation (CCC) or Federal Crop Insurance Corporation (FCIC) or any similar or successor organization or entity;

(g) To exercise or perform any act, power, duty, right or obligation whatsoever that I now have or may later acquire the legal right, power, or capacity to exercise or perform, in connection with, arising from, or relating to any person, item, transaction thing, business property, real or personal, tangible or intangible, or matter whatsoever;

(h) To resign any position I may hold as a director, officer, fiduciary or in any other capacity;

(i) To execute Federal or state income tax returns, gift tax returns or any other returns or forms, documents or agreements relating thereto or otherwise dealing with the IRS or any state agency involved in the collection or payment of any taxes;

(j) To open or maintain accounts with financial institutions and to buy, sell, endorse, transfer, hypothecate and borrow against any shares of stocks, bonds or other securities and to vote as my proxy any such shares;

(k) To make any and all arrangements deemed appropriate and in my best interest for my personal care, support maintenance, living arrangements and medical care, including admission to a hospital, retirement home or facility, extended care facility, nursing home, hospital or any other convalescent or medical care unless I have otherwise appointed another person as my attorney in fact for health care decisions, in which event such other appointment shall take precedence over this direction;

(l) To apply for Medicaid, Social Security, or any other publicly or privately funded assistance program, and to execute any documents and do any other acts deemed necessary or advisable to qualify me or make me eligible for such assistance. To enter into a Notice of Intent to Divide Resources or Income or both, Interspousal Agreement to Divide Resources or Income or both, or any document of similar purpose, in order to protect as many of my assets as possible from the spend-down requirements of eligibility for Medicaid and thus provide more income and resources to my spouse; to make any transfers to my spouse needed to carry out the terms of such Notice of Intent or other such documents; to make any transfers with or without consideration to my spouse or others (including transfer on any real estate which is my homestead); to sign a statement of my intent to return to my home in connection with any applications for Medicaid assistance for hospital, nursing home or extended health care, or for any other purpose; and to do any other matters necessary or advisable under all the circumstances (including but not limited to my situation and that of my spouse and family and appropriate estate planning for me and my spouse) to increase my eligibility for Medicaid, Social Security, or any other publicly or privately funded assistance program.

(m) To execute a power of attorney required by any governmental agency or other entity on my behalf naming my attorney in fact as the attorney in fact authorized to enter into any transaction with such agency or entity;

(n) To exercise authority over digital assets on my behalf including a catalogue of electronic communications sent or received by me but not the content of electronic communications unless specifically authorized as an optional additional power.

All acts done by my attorney in fact shall inure to my benefit and shall likewise bind me and my successors in interest.

OPTIONAL ADDITIONAL POWERS

(6) I grant my attorney in fact the authority to take the following actions but only to the extent that I have affirmatively expressed my intentions by initialing on the line designated "include" in front of the description of the power conveyed. If I have initialed the line designated "exclude" or if I have left both lines blank, then I do not intend to grant my attorney in fact the authority to take the action described.

	Include	Exclude	
(a)	_____	_____	To execute, amend or revoke any trust agreement.
(b)	_____	_____	To fund with my assets any trust not created by me.
(c)	_____	_____	To make or revoke a gift of my property in trust or otherwise.
(d)	_____	_____	To disclaim a gift or devise of property to or for my benefit.
(e)	_____	_____	To create or change survivorship interests in my property or in property in which I may have an interest.
(f)	_____	_____	To designate or change the designation of beneficiaries to receive any property, benefit or contract right upon my death.
(g)	_____	_____	To give or withhold consent to an autopsy or postmortem exam.
(h)	_____	_____	To make or decline to make a gift of my body parts under an anatomical gift act.
(i)	_____	_____	To nominate a guardian or conservator for me, and the attorney in fact may nominate himself or herself.
(j)	_____	_____	To give consent on my behalf to the sale, gift, transfer, mortgage or other alienation of my homestead or interest in my homestead. The street address of the homestead is: _____ _____, and the legal description of the homestead is:_____ _____ _____. Nothing in this document shall be construed as a limitation or abridgement of the right of my spouse to consent or withhold consent to the alienation of the spouse's homestead or any rights in the homestead, under Article 15, section 9 of the Kansas Constitution.
(k)	_____	_____	To designate one or more substitute or successor or additional attorneys in fact.
(l)	_____	_____	To delegate any or all powers contained in this document.
(m)	_____	_____	To exercise authority over the content of electronic communications sent or received by me pursuant to K.S.A. 58-4809.
(n)	_____	_____	To pay reasonable expenses incurred for my funeral and burial or other disposition of my body.

POWERS PROHIBITED

(7) As provided in K.S.A. 58-654(g) my attorney in fact shall not have the power or authority to do any of the following acts:

      (a) To make, publish, declare, amend or revoke my will;

      (b) Make, execute, modify or revoke a living will or "do not resuscitate" order or a durable power of attorney for health care decisions;

      (c) To require me, against my will, to take any action or to refrain from taking any action;

      (d) To carry out any action I have specifically forbidden while not under any disability or incapacity.

ACCOUNTING

(8) (Initial the following optional directives desired by the principal)

_____   I direct as soon as practicable after my death that my attorney in fact shall provide an accounting to my personal representative or trustee in such manner and for such period as requested by the personal representative or trustee.

_____   I direct as soon as practicable after my disability that my attorney in fact shall provide an accounting to _____.

_____   I waive the necessity of my attorney in fact providing an accounting to me or any other person during my lifetime or upon my death.

_____   (Here insert any other direction relating to accounting.) _____
_____
_____

This instrument is executed, delivered and shall be governed by the Kansas Power of Attorney Act, and amendments thereto and all questions as to its validity, powers of the attorney in fact and construction shall be likewise so governed.

_____   _____
       Signature of Principal   Date

State of Kansas

County of _____

This instrument was acknowledged before me on _____,

by _____.

_____
Notarial Officer
Title:_____

(SEAL)

My appointment expires:_____

ACCEPTANCE OF AUTHORITY AND AGREEMENT TO ACT

(Optional)

Now on this _____ day of _____, 20_____,

_____ attorney in fact,

accepts the authority granted in this document and agrees to act in the best interest of the
above named principal in carrying out the duties and responsibilities set forth in this
document until such time as said authority is terminated by the principal or by operation
of law, whichever occurs first.

State of Kansas

County of _____

This instrument was acknowledged before me on _____,

by _____.

_____

Notarial Officer

Title:_____

(SEAL)

My appointment expires:_____

CERTIFICATION BY ATTORNEY IN FACT

(Optional To Do Later Upon Request)

I, _____ (name of Attorney in Fact), certify under penalty of perjury that _____(name of Principal) granted me authority as an attorney in fact or successor attorney in fact in a power of attorney dated _____.

I further certify that to my knowledge:

(1) the Power of Attorney is durable, and the Principal is alive and has not revoked the Power of Attorney or my authority to act under the Power of Attorney, and the Power of Attorney and my authority to act under the Power of Attorney have not terminated;

(2) if the Power of Attorney was drafted to become effective upon the happening of an event or contingency, the event or contingency has occurred;

(3) if I was named as a successor attorney in fact, the prior attorney in fact is no longer able or willing to serve; and

(4) _____

_____

_____

(Insert other relevant statements)

SIGNATURE AND ACKNOWLEDGMENT

_____   _____
Attorney in Fact's Signature   Date

_____
Attorney in Fact's Name Printed

_____
Attorney in Fact's Address

_____
Attorney in Fact's Telephone

State of Kansas

County of _____

This document was acknowledged before me on _____, by
                                                              (Date)

_____
(Name of Attorney in Fact)

                                        _____
                                        Signature of Notarial Officer

                                        _____
                                        Title

(Seal, if any)
My appointment expires: _____

CHAPTER 15
FORM 9: DURABLE POWER OF ATTORNEY FOR HEALTH CARE AND EDUCATION RELATED DECISIONS (ABOUT CHILDREN)

FORM LETS PARENT SHARE POWER TO SOMEONE OVER CHILD UNDER 18

This form lets a parent of children under 18 share power over them to someone named in the form. This book's form is based on a popular form by a Kansas legal aid organization.

FORM CAN GIVE POWER TO SOMEONE OVER CHILD UNDER 18

In the form a parent called in the form the "Principal" can give some power over their children under 18 to a person they name who is called in the form the "Agent". The person who did the form can fire the Agent or overrule a decision. Often given power is a friend, teacher, or other family member helping watch a child. The form gives power over a child's health care and schooling, and these are the 2 areas that matter most to people and usually requires written proof. This form is sometimes used if parent or child is away from the other for work, school, training, drug treatment, sports, prison or jail, immigration, military, weeks long visit with family or friends, or if child is very sick in hospital. This form is sometimes done if a person watches a child periodically, like many times a month. The form is usually <u>not</u> done for brief situations like babysitter, daycare, week with relative, or anytime a parent can come quickly. Using this form may avoid need for more serious legal actions like legal guardianship or change of custody.

FORM IS SIGNED BY PARENT WITH A NOTARY

The form must be signed by a parent in front of a notary who then notarizes it. Some people modify the form to add a 2nd parent to make it likelier people trust the form. Once done some cautious people quickly show the form to schools and doctors to tell them they should follow it later. Note, unlike most states Kansas law doesn't clearly say these forms can be used to give power over children and some doctors and schools may not follow them, but someone watching a child having this form can be better than nothing. People who want to be more careful can go through the paperwork and time to ask a judge to name an official Temporary Guardian while parents are away. Once signed usually a parent gives the form to the person getting power. To cancel things a person should tell the Agent and maybe places that saw the form.

DURABLE POWER OF ATTORNEY FOR HEALTH CARE AND EDUCATION RELATED DECISIONS (ABOUT CHILDREN)

GENERAL STATEMENT OF AUTHORITY GRANTED

I, _____, the undersigned principal, hereby appoint _____ to act on my behalf, and to be agent for my minor children named here

Name:_____ **Date of Birth:**_____

Name:_____ **Date of Birth:**_____

Name:_____ **Date of Birth:**_____

Name:_____ **Date of Birth:**_____

Name:_____ **Date of Birth:**_____

and be agent for health care and education related decisions and pursuant to the language stated below, on my behalf to:

HEALTH CARE DECISIONS

1. Consent, refuse consent, or withdraw consent, concerning my minor children, to any care, treatment, service or procedure to maintain, diagnose or treat a physical or mental condition, and to make decisions about organ donation, autopsy and disposition of the body;

2. Make all necessary arrangements at any hospital, psychiatric hospital or psychiatric treatment facility, hospice, nursing home or similar institution; to employ or discharge health care personnel to include physicians, psychiatrists, psychologists, dentists, nurses, therapists or any other person who is licensed, certified or otherwise authorized or permitted by the laws of this state to administer health care as the agent shall deem necessary for the physical, mental and emotional well being of my minor children; and

3. Request, receive and review any information, verbal or written, regarding my minor children's personal affairs or physical or mental health including medical and hospital records and to execute any releases of other documents that may be required in order to obtain such information.

EDUCATION RELATED DECISIONS

     4. Serve as the decision maker in education related matters of my minor children, including, but not limited to: enrollment in secondary or post-secondary school or schools;

     5. Serve as the decision maker in any issues concerning my minor children, including, but not limited to transfers, transcripts, extra-curricular activities, special education, sports, field trips, parent teacher conferences, disciplinary action, progress reports, transportation, and attendance.

LIMITATIONS OF AUTHORITY

The powers of the agent herein shall be limited to the extent set out in writing in this durable power of attorney for health care and education related decisions, and shall not include the power to revoke or invalidate any previously existing declaration made in accordance with the natural death act.

EFFECTIVE TIME

This power of attorney for health care and education related decisions shall become effective immediately and shall not be affected by my subsequent disability or incapacity. The rights, powers, and authority granted herein shall remain in full force and effect thereafter until my death.

RELIANCE

Any party presented with a copy of this Durable Power of Attorney for Health Care and Education Related Decisions may rely upon such presentation as conclusive evidence of its present validity and effectiveness. No person who acts in reliance upon the representations of or the authority granted my agent shall incur any liability to me or to my estate as a result of permitting my agent to exercise any power.

Dated this _____ day of _____, 20___.

_____
Signature of Parent

ACKNOWLEDGEMENT TO
DURABLE POWER OF ATTORNEY
FOR HEALTH CARE AND EDUCATION RELATED DECISIONS

STATE OF KANAS   )

) SS.

COUNTY OF _____)

      Before me, the undersigned authority, on this day personally appeared _____ known to me to be the person executing this Durable Power of Attorney, whose name is subscribed to the foregoing instrument;

and, this person being by me first duly sworn did declare to me in my presence that the instrument, the Durable Power of Attorney for Health Care and Education Related Decisions, is for this person's minor children named in this document,

and this person has willingly made and executed it as this person's free and voluntary act and deed for the purposes therein expressed;

and that this person at that time possessed the rights of majority, was of sound mind, and under no restraint.

Subscribed and sworn to before me by _____, this _____ day of _____, 20 ____.

_____

NOTARY PUBLIC

My appointment expires:_____

APPENDIX: SAMPLE FILLED OUT FORMS

TO GET FORMS TO USE PEOPLE CAN:

(1) PHOTOCOPY BOOK PAGES,

(2) TEAR OUT PAGES FROM A BOOK, OR

(3) DOWNLOAD BOOK WITH FORMS FROM WWW.DAVENPORTPUBLISHING.COM AND USUALLY PDF FORM AT IS BEST TO AVOID SPACING/FORMAT CHANGES.

EMAIL ANY COMMENTS TO DAVENPORTPRESS@GMAIL.COM .

On the next pages to show how it can be done are some sample filled out legal forms.

People can add words to legal forms by computer or typewriter to be neater, but many people just by hand use pen, marker, or pencil to handwrite words into forms.

It is not required but is bit better if signatures are in ink or marker not pencil.

Many parts of the forms especially Will gifts can be left empty and unfilled.

Anyone can fill in words in legal form not just the person doing the form, like a friend with neat writing can fill in all the words, addresses, and dates that are needed. Only the final signatures must be done by each person who wants the form.

To add words in form by pen, pencil, typewriter, or computer any of these is fine:

"I appoint ___*John Doe*___ as Agent" ,

"I appoint ___John Doe___ as Agent",

"I appoint John Doe as Agent".

When doing forms it may help to know "respectively" means "in order just stated".

People need not worry about neatness or small mistakes, and a document is usually fine if those people who knew a decedent in life can tell the likely meaning.

Sample Filled Out Form: Last Will and Testament (Standard)
with Gifts section skipped to not bother making small gifts (which many people may
want to do especially if they have a spouse or young children)

LAST WILL AND TESTAMENT

I, <u>*Paul Thomas Maxwell*</u> , of <u>*Sedgwick County*</u> , Kansas, do revoke all prior Wills, Testaments, and Codicils, and do make, publish, and declare this as my Will. I am of sound mind and under no duress or undue influence and acting voluntarily.

1. GIFTS. I give these gifts in this Will, but to get a gift in this section the recipient must survive me except as otherwise stated below.

I give _____ to _____.

I give _____ to _____.

I give _____ to _____.

I give _____ to _____.

I give _____ to _____.

I give _____ to _____.

I give _____ to _____.

I give _____ to _____.

I give _____ to _____.

I give _____ to _____.

2. SEPARATE WRITINGS. I may do writings separate from this Will to gift tangible personal property as allowed by state law including Kansas Statutes 59-623, and all such writings should be followed. This Will does not revoke any such writings that now exist. A gift in such a writing to a person who does not survive me is canceled and has no effect. Any such writing not found within 90 days of my death is canceled and has no effect.

3. RESIDUE. I give the rest and residue and remainder of my estate, my money and property of any kind and nature, and anything I have an interest in so long as it was not transferred by other Will provisions (all of which is called the "residue"), as follows:

  a) to <u>*Susan Lee Maxwell*</u> who survive me with persons just named who survive me taking the share of non-survivors, then

  b) to <u>*Oscar David Maxwell and Jennifer Judy Tabor*</u> and if any of those just named do not survive me their part goes to their lineal descendants, per stirpes.

51

4. ADMINISTRATION. I name and appoint _____ *Susan Lee Maxwell* _____ as as Personal Representative including for me, my Will, and my estate.

5. MISCELLANEOUS. The following applies to this Will and generally.

My main residence is in Kansas and Kansas law should apply to this Will.

Priority of Will gifts of the same type is based on the order they are written.

In this document no unfilled part is a mistake and residue spaces may be left blank.

The words "give" and "gift" also means a devise, bequest, grant, legacy, or similar.

A gift of property no longer owned by Testator at death shall lapse and be of no effect including no payment of money shall be done in its place, all without ademption.

If a gift or section in this Will reasonably mentions survival in any way then survival is an absolute condition and anti-lapse laws or similar have no effect.

Unless a Will gift specifies otherwise if a Will gift goes to multiple recipients if any do not survive Testator their part to them lapses and instead goes to other surviving recipients.

Failure to make more or any Will gifts or other provisions to or for current children or a current spouse at the time I do this Will is intentional and not a mistake to remedy.

No gift or transfer I made during my life to a person reduces or offsets a Will gift, unless during my life I expressly usually called it a loan or advancement.

Unless another meaning is shown by context use of plural includes the singular and vice versa, and also masculine, feminine, and neuter words are used interchangeably. Unless another meaning is shown "they" means both one person and multiple persons.

Unless a Will specifically says otherwise a) a secured debt including a mortgage or lien shall not be paid off including by a Personal Representative or in probate, b) a recipient of a Will gift of property takes it subject to debts, c) no recipient of a Will gift who later loses property gifted to them to a debtor or who pays to avoid foreclosure or other loss may require the estate or anyone to pay recipient back, do exoneration, or do or pay anything.

I request and authorize any informal, summary, and quick probate or similar action. Any Personal Representative may act independently with no supervision of any court, including independent administration, and without doing any action or filings in court.

I give any Personal Representative a) the fullest authority, powers, and discretion that is allowed by state law, b) authority to lease, sell, mortgage, convey, or retain property including real property in any such manner and time they deem helpful or proper, and c) authority to settle or pay claims or debts at any time they in their sole discretion choose. Any Personal Representative shall also have all powers that may be given or held by law.

Any Personal Representative shall have sole discretion how to balance people's feelings and pick property or divide a gift to carry out a general gift or a gift to multiple persons.

If context permits the terms Personal Representative, Executor, and Administrator are interchangeable as if all were written, and Conservator is interchangeable with a Guardian

of the Estate or of Property. The terms Residue and Residuary also are interchangeable.

The residue includes lapsed or failed gifts, insurance paid to the estate, any inheritances owed, and property I have or had a power of appointment or testamentary disposition over.

Any Personal Representative, Executor, Administrator, Guardian, Conservator, Custodian, and any fiduciary under this Will or otherwise shall qualify and serve without bond, surety, security, surety bond, or similar.

If part of this Will is by law invalid or unenforceable other provisions remain in effect.

Any Personal Representative may at any time transfer money or property of a minor under age 18 to a Custodian to serve under the Kansas Uniform Transfers to Minors Act or a similar law anywhere. Any Personal Representative may select the Custodian including themselves but if they do not I name for this the person named Conservator in this Will.

TESTATOR

IN WITNESS WHEREOF, I, the Testator, publish, declare, and sign this instrument as my Will which I make voluntarily, and I have set my hand and seal on this Will on the _22nd_ day of _June_, 20_22_.

Paul Thomas Maxwell
Signature of Testator

WITNESSES

We, the persons who sign immediately below, do hereby certify and declare as follows:

the document above of which this paragraph is a part at the time and place stated in the document was freely and voluntarily signed and declared by _Paul Thomas Maxwell_, the Testator, to be the Testator's Will, in the presence of both of us;

that at the time of execution by Testator of this document the Testator was according to our best knowledge and belief of sound and disposing mind and memory and under no restraint; and

in the presence of each other and in Testator's presence and at the Testator's request we have now on the document signed our names as witnesses.

Dated at _Wichita_, Kansas, on the _22nd_ day of _June_, 20_22_.

Eve Mable Rogers   _14 2nd St., Wichita, KS 67201_
Signature of Witness   Address of Witness

Mary Ann Moon   _835 Buffalo Road, Boise, ID 83701_
Signature of Witness   Address of Witness

LAST WILL AND TESTAMENT

I, <u>Paul Brian Kent</u> , of <u>Wyandotte County</u> , Kansas, do revoke all prior Wills, Testaments, and Codicils, and do make, publish, and declare this as my Will. I am of sound mind and under no duress or undue influence and acting voluntarily.

1. GIFTS. I give these gifts in this Will, but to get a gift in this section the recipient must survive me except as otherwise stated below.

I give <u>big oak table</u> to <u>Anne J. Smith</u> .

I give <u>$5,000</u> to <u>Loretta Marsha Switt</u> .

I give <u>63 Ivy Road, Overland Park, Kansas</u> to <u>Kenneth Victor Poppler.</u>

I give <u>all real property and fixtures I own in Sedgwick County, Kansas</u> to <u>Amy Marie Fox</u> .

I give <u>903 Iceberg Road, Anchorage, Alaska</u> to <u>James Eric Hanson</u> .

I give <u>Bronze Roman Lamp</u> to <u>Anne Kilby</u> and <u>Kevin Kilby.</u>

I give <u>wedding ring</u> to <u>Ruth Jones.</u>

I give <u>all jewelry not given above</u> to <u>Kay Pidoski.</u>

I give <u>$781.35</u> to <u>Wanda Kay Zinski</u> .

I give <u>Wells Fargo acct ending in #8923</u> to <u>Lawrence Deer a hunting buddy</u> .

I give <u>1998 Ford truck</u> to <u>John Rupert Smith</u> .

I give <u>$200</u> to <u>Kent Food Shelf on Smith Road in Shawnee, Kansas</u> .

I give <u>all spare tires and auto parts I own</u> to <u>Victor Perez my mechanic</u> .

I give <u>$1000 each</u> to <u>each of my grandchildren</u> .

2. SEPARATE WRITINGS. I may do writings separate from this Will to gift tangible personal property as allowed by state law including Kansas Statutes 59-623, and all such writings should be followed. This Will does not revoke any such writings that now exist. A gift in such a writing to a person who does not survive me is canceled and has no effect. Any such writing not found within 90 days of my death is canceled and has no effect.

3. RESIDUE. I give the rest and residue and remainder of my estate, my money and property of any kind and nature, and anything I have an interest in so long as it was not transferred by other Will provisions (all of which is called the "residue"), as follows:

a) to _____ Ruth May Kent my wife _____ who survive me with persons just named who survive me taking the share of non-survivors, then

b) to 45% to Oscar Elliot Kent my son and 45% to Karen Lisa Lundy my daughter and 10% to Pedro Juan Sanchez and if any of those just named do not survive me their part goes to their lineal descendants, per stirpes.

4. ADMINISTRATION. I name and appoint ___ Ruth May Kent _____ as Personal Representative including for me, my Will, and my estate.

5. GUARDIAN. I name and appoint Karen Lisa Fox my sister ___ as Guardian of any minor child of mine including if needed to have care, authority, and custody of them. I also name and appoint this same person as Conservator for any minor child and the minor child's property, money, and estate.

6. MISCELLANEOUS. The following applies to this Will and generally.

My main residence is in Kansas and Kansas law should apply to this Will.

Priority of Will gifts of the same type is based on the order they are written.

The words "give" and "gift" also means a devise, bequest, grant, legacy, or similar.

A gift of property no longer owned by Testator at death shall lapse and be of no effect including no payment of money shall be done in its place, all without ademption.

If a gift or section in this Will reasonably mentions survival in any way then survival is an absolute condition and anti-lapse laws or similar have no effect.

Unless a Will gift specifies otherwise if a Will gift goes to multiple recipients if any do not survive Testator their part to them lapses and instead goes to other surviving recipients.

Failure to make more or any Will gifts or other provisions to or for current children or a current spouse at the time I do this Will is intentional and not a mistake to remedy.

No gift or transfer I made during my life to a person reduces or offsets a Will gift, unless during my life I expressly usually called it a loan or advancement.

Unless another meaning is shown by context use of plural includes the singular and vice versa, and also masculine, feminine, and neuter words are used interchangeably. Unless another meaning is shown "they" means both one person and multiple persons.

Unless a Will specifically says otherwise a) a secured debt including a mortgage or lien shall not be paid off including by a Personal Representative or in probate, b) a recipient of a Will gift of property takes it subject to debts, c) no recipient of a Will gift who later loses

property gifted to them to a debtor or who pays to avoid foreclosure or other loss may require the estate or anyone to pay recipient back, do exoneration, or do or pay anything.

Any Personal Representative shall have sole discretion how to balance people's feelings and pick property or divide a gift to carry out a general gift or a gift to multiple persons.

The residue includes lapsed or failed gifts, insurance paid to the estate, any inheritances owed, and property I have or had a power of appointment or testamentary disposition over.

Any Personal Representative, Executor, Administrator, Guardian, Conservator, Custodian, and any fiduciary under this Will or otherwise shall qualify and serve without bond, surety, security, surety bond, or similar.

If part of this Will is by law invalid or unenforceable other provisions remain in effect.

Any Personal Representative may at any time transfer money or property of a minor under age 18 to a Custodian to serve under the Kansas Uniform Transfers to Minors Act or a similar law anywhere. Any Personal Representative may select the Custodian including themselves but if they do not I name for this the person named Conservator in this Will.

TESTATOR

IN WITNESS WHEREOF, I, the Testator, publish, declare, and sign this instrument as my Will which I make voluntarily, and I have set my hand and seal on this Will on the 30th day of __December__, 20 _19_.

Paul Brian Kent
Signature of Testator

WITNESSES

We, the persons who sign immediately below, do hereby certify and declare as follows:

the document above of which this paragraph is a part at the time and place stated in the document was freely and voluntarily signed and declared by Paul Brian Kent___, the Testator, to be the Testator's Will, in the presence of both of us;

that at the time of execution by Testator of this document the Testator was according to our best knowledge and belief of sound and disposing mind and memory and under no restraint; and

in the presence of each other and in Testator's presence and at the Testator's request we have now on the document signed our names as witnesses.

Dated at Bonner Springs___, Kansas, on the 30th_ day of __December___, 20 _19_.

Olivia Joy Pawlenty	87 Forest Road, Topeka, KS 67045
Signature of Witness	Address of Witness
Roy Felix Pawlenty	87 Forest Road, Topeka, KS 67045
Signature of Witness	Address of Witness

LAST WILL AND TESTAMENT

I, **David Eric Smith**, of **East Haysville**, Kansas, do revoke all prior Wills, Testaments, and Codicils, and do make, publish, and declare this as my Will. I am of sound mind and under no duress or undue influence and acting voluntarily.

1. GIFTS. I give these gifts in this Will, but to get a gift in this section the recipient must survive me except as otherwise stated below.

I give ___ $500 ___ to _____ each of my brothers, sisters, and cousins _____ .

I give ___ $1000 ___ to _____ Baker Food Shelf on Fern Road in Overland Park, Kansas .

2. SEPARATE WRITINGS. I may do writings separate from this Will to gift tangible personal property as allowed by state law including Kansas Statutes 59-623, and all such writings should be followed. This Will does not revoke any such writings that now exist. A gift in such a writing to a person who does not survive me is canceled and has no effect. Any such writing not found within 90 days of my death is canceled and has no effect.

3. RESIDUE. The rest and residue and remainder of my estate, my property of any kind and nature, and anything I have an interest in, I give to **Adam Michael Smith and Ann Sue Baker who survive me** and to lineal descendants per stirpes of a person just named who did not survive me.

4. ADMINISTRATION. I name and appoint **Ann Sue Baker** as Personal Representative including for me, my Will, and my estate.

5. MISCELLANEOUS. The following applies to this Will and generally.
My main residence is in Kansas and Kansas law should apply to this Will.
Priority of Will gifts of the same type is based on the order they are written.
In this document no unfilled part is a mistake and residue spaces may be left blank.
The words "give" and "gift" also means a devise, bequest, grant, legacy, or similar.
A gift of property no longer owned by Testator at death shall lapse and be of no effect including no payment of money shall be done in its place, all without ademption.
If a gift or section in this Will reasonably mentions survival in any way then survival is an absolute condition and anti-lapse laws or similar have no effect.

57

Unless a Will gift specifies otherwise if a Will gift goes to multiple recipients if any do not survive Testator their part to them lapses and instead goes to other surviving recipients.

Failure to make more or any Will gifts or other provisions to or for current children or a current spouse at the time I do this Will is intentional and not a mistake to remedy.

No gift or transfer I made during my life to a person reduces or offsets a Will gift, unless during my life I expressly usually called it a loan or advancement.

Unless another meaning is shown by context use of plural includes the singular and vice versa, and also masculine, feminine, and neuter words are used interchangeably. Unless another meaning is shown "they" means both one person and multiple persons.

Unless a Will specifically says otherwise a) a secured debt including a mortgage or lien shall not be paid off including by a Personal Representative or in probate, b) a recipient of a Will gift of property takes it subject to debts, c) no recipient of a Will gift who later loses property gifted to them to a debtor or who pays to avoid foreclosure or other loss may require the estate or anyone to pay recipient back, do exoneration, or do or pay anything.

I request and authorize any informal, summary, and quick probate or similar action. Any Personal Representative may act independently with no supervision of any court, including independent administration, and without doing any action or filings in court.

I give any Personal Representative a) the fullest authority, powers, and discretion that is allowed by state law, b) authority to lease, sell, mortgage, convey, or retain property including real property in any such manner and time they deem helpful or proper, and c) authority to settle or pay claims or debts at any time they in their sole discretion choose. Any Personal Representative shall also have all powers that may be given or held by law.

Any Personal Representative shall have sole discretion how to balance people's feelings and pick property or divide a gift to carry out a general gift or a gift to multiple persons.

If context permits the terms Personal Representative, Executor, and Administrator are interchangeable as if all were written, and Conservator is interchangeable with a Guardian of the Estate or of Property. The terms Residue and Residuary also are interchangeable.

The residue includes lapsed or failed gifts, insurance paid to the estate, any inheritances owed, and property I have or had a power of appointment or testamentary disposition over.

Any Personal Representative, Executor, Administrator, Guardian, Conservator, Custodian, and any fiduciary under this Will or otherwise shall qualify and serve without bond, surety, security, surety bond, or similar.

If part of this Will is by law invalid or unenforceable other provisions remain in effect.

Any Personal Representative may at any time transfer money or property of a minor under age 18 to a Custodian to serve under the Kansas Uniform Transfers to Minors Act or a similar law anywhere. Any Personal Representative may select the Custodian including themselves but if they do not I name for this the person named Conservator in this Will.

TESTATOR

IN WITNESS WHEREOF, I, the Testator, publish, declare, and sign this instrument as my Will which I make voluntarily, and I have set my hand and seal on this Will on the **21st** day of **June**, 2021.

David Eric Smith
Signature of Testator

WITNESSES

We, the persons who sign immediately below, do hereby certify and declare as follows:

the document above of which this paragraph is a part at the time and place stated in the document was freely and voluntarily signed and declared by **David Eric Smith** the Testator, to be the Testator's Will, in the presence of both of us;

that at the time of execution by Testator of this document the Testator was according to our best knowledge and belief of sound and disposing mind and memory and under no restraint; and

in the presence of each other and in Testator's presence and at the Testator's request we have now on the document signed our names as witnesses.

Dated at **East Haysville,** Kansas, on the **21st** day of **June**, 2021.

Harriet Potter
Signature of Witness

204 Main Street, Olathe, KS 67286
Address of Witness

Ann Paula Blom
Signature of Witness

27 Dog River Road, Gresham, CT 06823
Address of Witness

SELF-PROVING AFFIDAVIT

State of Kansas   )
) ss.

County of _Sedgwick_   )

Before me, the undersigned authority, on this day personally appeared _David Eric Smith_, _Harriet Potter_ and _Ann Paula Blom_, known to me to be the Testator and the witnesses, respectively, whose names are subscribed to the annexed or foregoing instrument in their respective capacities, and, all of such persons being by me first duly sworn, such _David Eric Smith_, Testator, declared to me and to the witnesses in my presence that such instrument is the Testator's Will, and that the Testator had willingly made and executed it as the Testator's free and voluntary act and deed for the purposes therein expressed. Such witnesses, each on the witness' oath stated to me, in the presence and hearing of the Testator, that the Testator had declared to them that such instrument is the Testator's Will, and that the Testator executed same as such and wanted each witness to sign it as a witness. Upon their oaths each witness stated further that they did sign the will as witnesses in the presence of each other and in the presence of the Testator and at the Testator's request, and that the Testator at that time possessed the rights of majority, was of sound mind, and under no restraint.

David Eric Smith
Testator's Signature

Harriet Potter
Witness Signature

Ann Paula Blom
Witness Signature

Subscribed, acknowledged and sworn to before me by _David Eric Smith_, Testator, and _Harriet Potter_ and _Ann Paula Blom_ witnesses, this _21st_ day of _June_, 20_21_.

(seal, if any)

NOTARY PUBLIC - State of Kansas
SANDRA H. FERNANDEZ
My Appt. Expires May. 18, 2037

Signed: **Sandra H. Hernandez**

Official Capacity of Officer: **Notary**

TANGIBLE PERSONAL PROPERTY LIST

In this writing are gifts of tangible personal property to occur after my death, but this writing if not found by someone within 90 days of my death is canceled.

I may do multiple pages of these writings which should be seen as a single document with the more recently done page controlling if any gifts conflict.

If a person getting a gift below does not survive me such gift is void and canceled.

PROPERTY ITEMS		NAMES OF RECIPIENTS
1998 Ford Truck	to	Samantha Bell
1.3 carat diamond ring + Irish rings	to	Ann Sue Reed
14 ft power boat + kayak + paddles	to	L. Wheeler
Amish style bench	to	Reba Stewart
glass table, telescope, umbrellas	to	Rebecca Stewart
Irish wood cups, oak platter, red vase	to	Mary and Cindy Lott
painting of sailboat in storm	to	Mary Lott
chainsaw marked with 382937	to	Mary Lott
chainsaw marked with 89930	to	Matt Smith
antique lanterns + repair kits	to	Sue Wu maid at Hart Hotel
oak lamp kept on porch	to	Mary Kay Poppler
sewing machines	to	Mary Kay Poppler
rocking chair bought in Oregon	to	Don Winkler boat mechanic
all fishing poles and fishing nets	to	Joe "Fish" Hoss, fishing pal
hats at cabin	to	Ken Baker
	to	
	to	
	to	
	to	

DATE: 2-12-2023   SIGNED: *David Eric Smith*